THE CRUSADES
AN EPITOME

SUSANNA A. THROOP

KISMET PRESS
MMXVIII | EPITOMES IV

The Crusades

AN EPITOME

Susanna A. Throop

kısmet·press

Libera Scientia | Free Knowledge

The Crusades: An Epitome
by Susanna A. Throop

Epitomes, 4
Series Editors: Tim Barnwell & N. Kıvılcım Yavuz

Published in 2018
by Kismet Press LLP
Kismet Press LLP
15 Queen Square, Leeds, LS2 8AJ, UK
kismet.press
kismet@kismet.press

Downloadable .epub edition also available

Printed and bound by IngramSpark with acid-free paper, using
a print-on-demand model with printers in the US, EU, and
Australia

A catalogue record for this book is available from the British
Library

ISBN 978-1-912801-02-2 (pbk)
ISBN 978-1-912801-03-9 (ebk)

For S. Ross Doughty
&
Reverend Charles William Rice
(1957–2017)

Contents

List of Maps

Acknowledgements

MY THANKS GO FIRST TO KISMET PRESS, IN PARTICULAR my editor, Tim Barnwell, and Kıvılcım Yavuz. I deeply appreciate both their commitment to scholarly Open Access publishing and the ease and pleasure of working with them. Generous thanks, too, to Ursinus College, which greatly expedited the writing of the book by providing a sabbatical semester, to the Andrew W. Mellon Foundation and Gates Cambridge Scholarship Programme, which enabled my graduate education , and to Jonathan Riley-Smith (1938–2016), PhD supervisor, mentor, and inspiration, who is always in my thoughts. I would particularly like to thank Ross Doughty, who has unfailingly celebrated my research and writing as a senior colleague and former department chair, and Charles Rice, who by word and example urged me to use my voice and inspired me to be my best self. I am indebted to them both. I am likewise deeply grateful to Morgan Larese and Elijah Sloat, my research assistants, and to the Ursinus College Student Research Assistantships in the

Humanities Program that supported their work. Morgan and Elijah helped me conceptualize and plan the book and their active collaboration, insightful questions, and critical feedback were invaluable.

A book like this that attempts to range so widely can only be written with content and insight from many, many others. This book rests on the scholarship of others and, equally, on the generous feedback of colleagues who took the time to read drafts and help me improve and correct the book. My heartfelt thanks go to Megan Cassidy-Welch, Peter Frankopan, Matthew Gabriele, M. Cecilia Gaposchkin, Jonathan Harris, Norman Housley, Katherine Lewis, Elizabeth Macaulay Lewis, Helen Nicholson, Nicholas Morton, Carol Symes, and Christopher Tyerman, as well as to my anonymous peer reviewer, who was clearly (and thankfully) a historian of the Islamic world. To review a book manuscript as they did requires time, energy, and goodwill, and I'm profoundly grateful and humbled that they helped me make this book better. Any and all errors, infelicities, and authorial choices are fully my own.

Every day I am grateful to my family for the love and happiness of our life together which also made this book possible. My love and appreciation go to my spouse, Matthew Abbott, to our three cats, Gemma, Rowan, and Sydney, and to all the members of my extended family who share laughter, love, and encouragement.

Note on Terminology
and Usage

ALL DATES PROVIDED WITHIN THE BOOK ARE COMMON
Era (CE) unless otherwise noted. Place names are given
in modern English. Personal names have been simplified,
standardized, and transliterated; I have minimized the use
of non-Latin symbols and have only used words in their
original language when to translate them would obscure
meaning. My hope is that these measures help make this
book accessible for an English-reading general audience.

I have tried to be as precise and consistent as possible
in describing peoples, regions, polities, and religions.
The task has not been easy, since our modern categories
for identity and geography do not map smoothly onto
the past. Furthermore, medieval cultural, religious, and
political identities did not necessarily align neatly with
each other.

I have aimed to describe political powers as specifically
as possible, and when discussing broader regional trends,

to use basic, though modern, geographical terms—i.e., northeastern Europe, north Africa, west Asia, eastern Mediterranean, and so on. Thus "Europe" always means the continent and "Latin Christian" always means the religion and neither term should be read as shorthand for the other, nor for race or other identity categories. Similarly "Iberia" refers to the geographical area of the Iberian Peninsula and "Anatolia" to the geographical area of the Anatolian peninsula; neither implies a specific religious, ethnic, or political unit.

When it comes to religious identity, writing from my own perspective as a historian, I discuss "Latin Christians" (i.e., members of the church of Rome) and "Byzantine Christians" as well as "Christian 'heretics.'" "Heretics" is almost always in quotation marks to signal that the accuracy of the term depends heavily on perspective. "Islam," "Muslim," and "Islamic" refer to the religion, while "Islamicate" refers to regions, groups, or polities in which Muslims (of whatever ethnicity or culture) were politically dominant. "Christendom" refers to the medieval concept of an ideal Christian society, a fully unified and homogenous politico-religious community.

There is a strong case to be made for using the (multiple) medieval terms for regions and locations, and there is an equally strong case for acknowledging that there are different traditions of geographic terminology around the world. However, given the plurality of perspectives I am attempting to synthesize, and thus the possibility of having to explain multiple names for each location, such an approach seemed inadvisable for a book of this length. I encourage all readers to explore elsewhere the rich and varied legacies of place names, personal names, and identity categories present in both the premodern and modern worlds.

Introduction: What Were the Crusades?

"As the poster conflict of civilizational clash, the history of the Crusades is an ideal subject for the foregrounding of [an informed dialogue between the West and the Muslim world]. In the final analysis, civilizations are not monoliths pitting different cultures in mutually antagonistic postures but a shifting landscape of units that cooperate or clash."[1]

THE FIRST CRUSADE (1096–99) MARCHED OVERLAND from Europe to the eastern Mediterranean, where its participants conquered the city of Jerusalem by force.

1   Umej Bhatia, *Forgetting Osama bin Munqidh, Remembering Osama bin Laden: The Crusades in Modern Muslim Memory* (Singapore: S. Rajaratnam School of International Studies, 2008), 65.

These first crusaders established a number of small states in the region, which they then struggled to defend and expand. As years, decades, and centuries rolled by, some sought to emulate the crusaders, while others in turn resisted their efforts. All the while, a variety of different voices strove to explain, celebrate, or condemn those who claimed to crusade.

Put that way, the history of the crusades seems remarkably simple. But in fact, the history of the crusades is complex and contested. It is contested in the twenty-first century; it was contested in the eighteenth, nineteenth, and twentieth centuries; and as this book demonstrates, it was contested in the twelfth century. While the events of the crusades may be relatively easy to pin down, the meanings ascribed to those events are slippery indeed. As a result, it is impossible to discuss the history of the crusades without discussing the nature of historical knowledge, as well as how the crusades have become so central and yet so disputed in modern conversations.

To begin, then, historians are unable to directly access the past. In the case of the First Crusade, for example, we cannot ourselves see Jerusalem conquered in 1099 or know with absolute certainty what passed in the minds of those who were there. We have access, instead, to a variety of different forms of historical evidence—texts, physical objects, architecture, archaeological remains. This evidence is always incomplete, due to the physical ravages of time and environment as well as decisions about what to keep and what to toss made by previous generations. The evidence is also always biased—that is, it reflects the perspectives of those who shaped it. After all, what we consider "historical evidence" was created to suit the wants and needs of its own time, not the priorities or perspectives of modern historians. Thus, while historians like to make claims about what "the evidence says," evidence always has to be interpreted, and it rarely speaks with a singular voice.

The task of the historian, then, is to ask questions about the past and to arrive at an answer based upon an interpretation of as much evidence as possible. Interpretations that are supported by the widest range of evidence and accepted by the overwhelming majority of historians—that are virtually incontrovertible—are deemed historical fact. Interpretations that are more recent or less widely accepted, or simply cannot be conclusively confirmed, are historical arguments. Thus historical knowledge, our understanding of the past, changes over time as historians accept or reject arguments, find new evidence, interpret old evidence differently, and ask other questions.

While historians strive for objectivity and transparency, both the questions they ask and the way they interpret evidence are unavoidably influenced by their own social context as well as their personal background. As a result, historical knowledge depends upon not only the intellectual rigor and ethics of individual historians, but also the commitment of historians, as a whole, to critical analysis and counterargument. History isn't written in stone, but neither is it an assortment of personal opinions; rather, it is a rigorous and ongoing attempt to understand the past on its own terms. The critical rigor of the field— including a commitment to avoid anachronism, nostalgia, and teleology—distinguish the study of history from general social memory. That historians, as human beings, do not always live up to these high expectations does not alter the fact that the expectations are firmly in place.

What does all this have to do with the crusades? Let's start with the term "crusade." The Latin term that can be translated as "crusader" first appears circa 1200, a century after the First Crusade. Even then, the Latin term—and its vernacular equivalents—were not always used consistently; one historical source might refer to "crusaders" while another might not. Admittedly, there can be a distinct phenomenon without a correlating term, and historians can study something that was not discretely identified in its own time. For example, a historian might analyze the "economic implications of tax reform" within a past society that never itself explicitly considered "the economic implications of tax reform," and that might not even have had a concept of "economics" as a distinct aspect of human life. Similarly, we can study "crusades" even if there was no term for it at a given moment, provided we agree on what "crusades" were. That last clause is key: any attempt to study the crusades, or tell the story of the crusades, is unavoidably based on historical arguments about what the crusades were. These arguments have been heated in part because the historical evidence is diverse and (of course) open to interpretation.

But historical arguments about the crusades have also been heated because the arguments have been politically charged and intimately connected to the perspectives and priorities of scholars and their times. For example, for David Hume, an eighteenth-century British intellectual, the crusades were the worst example of irrational zealotry that he believed preceded Europe's Enlightenment; for him, the crusades were "the most signal and most durable monument of human folly that has yet appeared in any age."[2] In contrast, for Joseph Michaud, a nineteenth-century French historian, the crusades were a glorious and heroic national enterprise that did (and should) fuel French patriotism.[3] Both Michaud and Sayyid Qutb, a mid-twentieth-century Egyptian intellectual, linked the crusades to modern European imperialism, but while Michaud celebrated this, Qutb condemned it.[4]

Such connections between historians' own societies, identities, and arguments, and the political charge that accompanies history, is not surprising—history is written by human beings—but it is worth noting. Because of these connections, the history of the crusades has been linked variously to nationalism, imperialism, irrationality, and racism, as well as to heroism, glory, piety, and triumphalism. As scholar and diplomat Umej Bhatia has noted, the crusades continue to be seen as the "poster conflict" for an incredibly wide variety of polemical

---

2   David Hume, *The History of England from the Invasion of Julius Caesar to the Abdication of James the Second, 1688* (Boston: Aldine Book Publishing, 1754–61), 226.

3   Joseph François Michaud, *The History of the Crusades*, trans. William Robson, 3 vols. (New York: A. C. Armstrong & Son, 1900), 1: 257.

4   Sayyid Qutb, *Social Justice in Islam*, trans. John B. Hardie, rev. ed. (Oneonta: Islamic Publications International, 2000), 269.

positions, all based on the idea of a seemingly eternal, inescapable, and historically inaccurate "civilizational clash."[5] Thus, the crusades can be invoked so variously and debated so heatedly precisely because of their malleability, and because of their ability to represent many different conjunctions of religion, violence, nationalism, and identity. This is the intense context in which the history of the crusades has been studied and written.

This is also the intense context in which this book has been written, and it has led me to not only make quite specific authorial choices, but to consider it imperative to communicate those choices to you, my readers, as clearly as I can. After all, any historical narrative is a combination of historical facts and historical arguments, and the specific combination depends upon the author's purpose. But this is especially true for a book such as this, which seeks to summarize centuries of hotly contested history in a very few pages. Writing this book has inevitably required that I make tough decisions about what to include and exclude, and I want to be direct about the arguments that I have used to build this book's narrative.

To begin, and to return to the problem of defining "crusades," this book is premised upon a pluralist definition of crusading. Pluralism, a school of thought outlined by historian Jonathan Riley-Smith among others,

---

5 Bhatia, *Forgetting Osama bin Munqidh, Remembering Osama bin Laden*, 65. The idea of this civilizational clash is represented in Samuel P. Huntington, *The Clash of Civilizations and the Remaking of World Order* (New York: Simon & Schuster, 1996).

reflects one of the biggest turns in the academic study of the crusades in the late twentieth century. Pluralism asserts that crusades were a subcategory of Christian holy war, which was in turn a subcategory of Christian just war. Crucially, it asserts that crusades could be distinguished from other Christian holy and just wars not by geography, target, or chronology, but rather by a number of key procedural elements, such as papal authorization. Thus, from a pluralist perspective, the crusades were not simply about Christians fighting Muslims for control of Jerusalem. Instead, as this book emphasizes, crusades were fought against Muslims, pagans, purported heretics, and political adversaries of the papacy, and crusades were fought around the Mediterranean, in Europe, and in Africa. In addition, while Jerusalem clearly served as both a literal and symbolic goal for many crusaders, it was not a *sine qua non* for crusading. Having said all that, pluralism does not noticeably distinguish this book from others, since at this point in time, a pluralist definition of crusading has been largely accepted by scholars.

What is more distinctive about this book is a central focus on historical complexity. Attention to complexity has guided my authorial decisions in three key ways. First, I have adopted a more global and less Eurocentric perspective on the crusades. In other words, I have aimed to locate crusading within the broader history of the eastern hemisphere, particularly the Mediterranean region, and to incorporate evidence and perspectives from different medieval cultures and historical traditions. Second, I have striven to acknowledge the diversity of historical actors and perspectives, to underline both continuity and change, and to firmly push against any idea of historical inevitability. Third, and following on this, one of the book's overall claims is that while there have been voices describing crusading as an epic "civilizational clash" since the eleventh century, equally there has always been another history visible and articulated by historical sources—one characterized by diplomacy, strategy, rhetoric, Realpolitik, exchange, conflict, transaction— in other words, a history colored in a wide spectrum of grays. Modern accounts of crusading are varied and contested, but so too were perspectives on crusading in the Middle Ages.

Attention to complexity has furthermore led to two characteristics of this book that should be highlighted in advance. This is not a military history of the crusades. You will learn here about an ambiguous and evolving phenomenon—"crusading"—rather than a series of discrete military campaigns. Similarly, while I do indicate in passing the nineteenth-century European numbering of crusades—First Crusade, Second Crusade, and so on—I do not otherwise use these numerical labels, with the exception of the First Crusade. On the one hand, I accept there is sufficient historical evidence to continue to represent the expedition of 1096–99 as a pivotal moment in the history of Christian warfare. On the other hand, the nineteenth-century numbering of crusades is potentially quite misleading when combined with a pluralist approach.

The net result of my attention to complexity is a new narrative history of the crusades. In terms of the book's structure, the chapters are balanced in length and proceed in loose chronological order. Chapter 1 explores the eastern hemisphere, Mediterranean, and Europe in the eleventh century to establish a broad context for the First Crusade. Chapter 2 analyzes the events of the First Crusade, as well as reactions to it, up to the mid-twelfth century. Chapter 3 puts crusading in the eastern Mediterranean into broader context by situating it within ongoing regional developments. Chapter 4 dives more deeply into Christendom, outlining key cultural themes in crusading and clarifying the role of intra-Christian crusades. Chapter 5 returns to the Mediterranean, a region in flux once again thanks to the arrival of new actors, while Chapter 6 showcases the persistent nature of crusading and its relationship with early modern Christian nationalism in Europe. In the conclusion, I briefly visit the various images of the crusades that have been invoked into the twenty-first century and make a final case for the value of historical complexity.

Each chapter begins with a short introduction that summarizes the previous chapter and outlines the main points to come. In line with the format of this book series, footnotes have been deliberately kept extremely minimal and instead, a short (and not comprehensive) list for suggested further reading is provided at the end of each chapter. Maps have been provided to support points made by the text. The length of the book corresponds to the standards of this book series; its length makes it inevitable that I will have left out things that matter to some and included things that seem less important to others. In making final revisions on a short timeline, regrettably I have been unable to incorporate a number of recent and pertinent publications, most especially Michael Lower's *The Tunis Crusade of 1270* and Geraldine Heng's *The Invention of Race in the European Middle Ages*, which includes a chapter related to the crusades.[6]

Furthermore, while I have done my very best to limit extraneous detail and unnecessary jargon, the book has been written with the assumption that you, my readers, are both intelligent and curious, and that most of you will be readily able and willing to access additional information online or in print. In other words, my hope is not that you read this book in isolation or as a sole authority, but rather, that it inspires you to seek out further knowledge and different perspectives, to engage in dialogue with others about the material, and to ask your own questions about the history of the crusades.

6   Michael Lower, *The Tunis Crusade of 1270: A Mediterranean History* (Oxford: Oxford University Press, 2018); Geraldine Heng, *The Invention of Race in the European Middle Ages* (Cambridge: Cambridge University Press, 2018).

Further Reading

Housley, Norman. *Contesting the Crusades*. Oxford: Wiley-Blackwell, 2006.

Riley-Smith, Jonathan. *What Were the Crusades?* 4th ed. San Francisco, Basingstoke, and New York: Ignatius Press and Palgrave MacMillan, 2009.

Tyerman, Christopher. *The Debate on the Crusades*. Manchester: Manchester University Press, 2011.

Note: Readers interested in primary sources in English translation have many options available to them. Some sources and excerpts are available online, in particular via the *Internet Medieval Sourcebook* (https://sourcebooks. fordham.edu/sbook.asp) and *De Re Militari* (https:// deremilitari.org/).

There are also a number of printed primary source collections; I have listed only a few here:

Allen, S. J., and Emilie Amt, eds. *The Crusades: A Reader*. 2nd ed. Toronto: University of Toronto Press, 2014.

Bird, Jessalyn, Edward Peters, and James M. Powell, eds. *Crusade and Christendom: Annotated Documents in Translation from Innocent III to the Fall of Acre, 1187–1291*. Philadelphia: University of Pennsylvania Press, 2014.

Eidelberg, Shlomo. *The Jews and the Crusaders: The Hebrew Chronicles of the First and Second Crusades*. Madison: University of Wisconsin Press, 1978.

Gabrieli, Francesco, ed. *Arab Historians of the Crusades*. Trans. E. J. Costello. Oxon: Routledge, 1969.

Peters, Edward, ed. *The First Crusade: "The Chronicle of Fulcher of Chartres" and Other Source Materials*. 2nd ed. Philadelphia: University of Pennsylvania Press, 1998.

There are also short histories of the crusades that incorporate translated sources. Again, I list only a few representative titles here:

Christie, Niall. *Muslims and Crusaders. Christianity's Wars in the Middle East, 1095–1382, from the Islamic Sources*. Oxon: Routledge, 2014.

Rubenstein, Jay. *The First Crusade: A Brief History with Documents*. Boston: Bedford/St. Martin's, 2015.

Lastly, many translated sources have been published in their entirety as single texts via Penguin Classics or the Crusades Texts in Translation Series (Routledge).

I

Connections and Conflicts in the Eleventh-Century Mediterranean

THE FIRST CRUSADE OCCURRED IN A COMPLEX AND dynamic eastern hemisphere, and it was strongly influenced by both longstanding trends and more recent events. Indeed, as one would expect, it wasn't called the "first" of anything at the time it happened. It was only in hindsight that the First Crusade became a beginning, and even in hindsight, it marked a beginning only in the eyes of some. Others at the time interpreted it as just another instance of phenomena already well underway.

This chapter provides historical context for the rise of the crusading movement. Our view will gradually narrow as we zoom in from Afro-Eurasia to the Mediterranean to Europe. As we'll see, the First Crusade, though impactful, was neither inevitable nor entirely new.

***

The eastern hemisphere was a large and relatively mobile place in the year 1000. Networks that allowed for the movement of ideas, wealth, and people spanned Afro-Eurasia. In east Asia, the prosperous, booming, and technologically sophisticated Song Dynasty in China was a—if not the—major engine of hemispheric growth. Well-travelled sea routes connected east Asia, south Asia, west Asia, and east Africa. Overland routes, meanwhile, connected Asia from east to west. Goods, technologies, conflicts, and cultures moved along these routes in both directions. People moved along these routes, too, both voluntarily and involuntarily; a demand for slave labor also connected many parts of the hemisphere.

Centrally located on these sea and land routes, poised between the eastern and western edges of the hemisphere, stretched a vast region that will here be called the Islamicate world. Although the religion of Islam and the Arabs as a people had expanded out from the Arabian peninsula dramatically in the seventh and eighth centuries, the Islamicate world circa 1000 was not unified or homogenous in terms of political powers, ethnic identities, or religious sects. Indeed, it was not exclusively populated by Muslims. While conversions to Islam continued to increase over time in areas under Islamic rule, the rulers of regions within the Islamicate

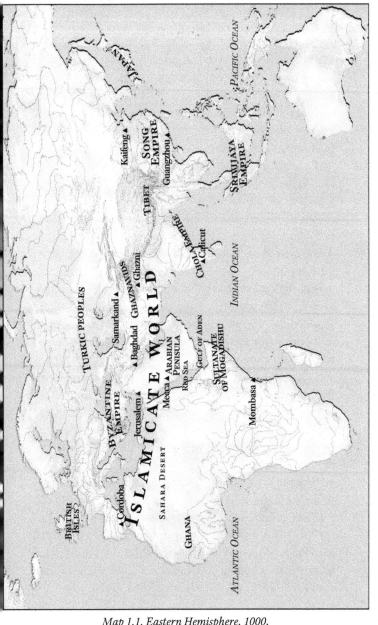

Map 1.1. Eastern Hemisphere, 1000.

world governed diverse and often non-Muslim-majority populations. These populations included members of many different Christian and Jewish sects, who were considered *dhimmis* ("protected persons"), socially inferior and subject to specific taxation in return for toleration and the protection of the ruler.

Despite all these variables, these regions shared four general characteristics that allow us to view them together as an Islamicate world. First, they shared common philosophies of Islamic government, as well as a common language for trade and intellectual work: Arabic. Second, they focused on the cultivation of prosperous and interconnected urban societies. Although people depended on technologically-assisted agriculture as the foundation of their economies—as everyone did at the time—the Islamicate world was distinctly urban in its priorities and achievements. Third, in many cases rulers were committed to fostering artistic, intellectual, and technological achievement, enabled by the material wealth generated by strong economies and expressed in the cities and courts of the elites. Lastly, many people in these regions valued trade and travel. Even armchair travelers avidly consumed guidebooks and maps, and the most adventurous explorers clocked up journeys of thousands of miles. These commonalities allow us to identify and discuss an Islamicate world despite the political, ethnic, and religious variation within it.

The Islamicate world played a vital role circa 1000 because it connected virtually the entirety of the eastern hemisphere. Looking east and south from Baghdad, one could travel far and wide: through the Red Sea and the

Gulf of Aden to the prosperous cities of the east African coast and the Indian Ocean; via the Indian Ocean to the thriving societies and markets of southeast and east Asia; by overland routes to the cities and markets of central and ultimately east Asia. Looking west from Baghdad, one could range across the Sahara to the wealthy kingdoms of west Africa or sail all around the Mediterranean, stopping at some ports governed by Muslims and others by Christians. The position of the Islamicate world vis-à-vis the rest of Afro-Eurasia allowed, in theory, for movement all the way from the prosperous kingdoms of western Africa—or the distant reaches of the British Isles—to Japan. The Islamicate world was thus, in a sense, the center of the eastern hemisphere as it existed in 1000. It was, however, a fluid and at times conflicted center, and the eleventh century proved to be particularly dynamic in the Mediterranean, the region with which this book is primarily concerned.

The medieval Mediterranean inherited the multiethnic and pluralistic legacy of the Roman Empire, as well as the legacies of all the many different peoples who had moved through the Roman Empire in late antiquity. (Indeed, the movement of peoples within Afro-Eurasia has a long, long history.) The medieval Mediterranean was thus populated by incredibly diverse yet interconnected human beings.

In the eleventh century, Christians, Muslims, and Jews all called communities around the Mediterranean home, living together in some places and apart in others. At the same time, Christian and Islamic communities had their own sectarian divisions. In eleventh-century Islam, the Sunni and Shiʿite divide was not necessarily explosive, and thus Sunnis and Shi'ites—as well as other Islamic sects—often coexisted in close proximity. Nonetheless the divide between Sunni and Shi'ite Islam could be a point of contention, particularly when sectarian allegiances aligned (or failed to align) with ethnic identity, economic interest, or political ambition. Eleventh-century Christianity also contained sectarian differences, perhaps most notably between the Latin church of Rome and the Byzantine church based at Constantinople. Additionally, many Christian sects that were considered heretical by both Latin and Byzantine churches continued to thrive in areas under Islamic rule.

Clearly, conflict existed within as well as between religions, and at times, both kinds of conflict were influenced by different traditions of holy war. Both Latin and Byzantine Christians had access to a clear tradition of approved Christian violence and just war from late antiquity forward. Justified Christian violence (including warfare), as influentially outlined by Augustine of Hippo in the late fourth and early fifth centuries, fulfilled three criteria: it responded to an injury; it was performed by an appropriate authority; and it was performed with correct intention. That correct intention was Christian love, i.e., charity (*caritas*); this love was supposed to lead Christians to seek the spiritual good of their adversaries (by forcibly correcting them) and to safeguard the spiritual wellbeing of Christendom. Meanwhile, Muslims had access to the concept of military *jihad*. While *jihad* (literally meaning "struggle") could be performed in a variety of different ways—most especially within oneself, against sin—it could also take the form of armed endeavor against enemies of Islam, i.e., military *jihad*. Both Christian and Muslim traditions of holy warfare could be directed at "internal" threats, i.e., other Christians or other Muslims.[7]

However, it is worth emphasizing vigorously that holy warfare was only one (and by no means the most regular) way that people interacted with each other in the eleventh-century Mediterranean. Then as now, people had choices about how they engaged with one another. Holy war was one choice; other modes of warfare and violence were also options; and so were coexistence, collaboration, diplomacy, intermarriage, and trade. Holy war was emphatically not some sort of default option for either Christians or Muslims, and whether religious similarities or differences sparked conflict or cooperation depended heavily on other contextual factors. As much of the rest of this book will show, religious accord did not necessarily lead to alliance and religious divisions did not necessarily lead to violence.

Moreover, religion was not the only aspect of identity that mattered in the eleventh century. People around the Mediterranean sought identity in ethnic and family groups as well as in religion or sect. In a world without nation-states in the modern sense, it was often kin identities that were most closely linked with political and economic activities. Familial, political, and economic relationships were often one and the same.

7 Those seeking a very succinct and clear comparison of Christian holy war and *jihad* are encouraged to consult Paul M. Cobb, *The Race for Paradise: An Islamic History of the Crusades* (Oxford: Oxford University Press, 2015), 29.

Most importantly, the eleventh-century Mediterranean was not static in any way. As the next section discusses, it was frequently, one is tempted to say incessantly, contested and traversed by actors large and small who shifted political alliances along or across religious or ethnic boundaries as it suited them. Economically, in a world where the fastest mode of travel was by sea, the Mediterranean was a superhighway, connecting the lands around it and providing access to further regions via the Sahara, the Red Sea, the Indian Ocean, and overland routes in Asia. From a religious perspective, the holiest cities of Jews, Christians, and Muslims were positioned on or just beyond the Mediterranean's eastern shore. And in the eleventh century, in particular, the Mediterranean witnessed the major influx and movement of several different mobile groups, from Saljuq Turks to Scandinavian Vikings and their descendants, the Normans. Surveying the basic political players in the medieval Mediterranean will allow us to better understand the complex dynamics of the region in the eleventh century.

The political situation in the eastern Mediterranean circa 1000 was complex and openly contested. In the early part of the eleventh century, Sunni 'Abbasid caliphs remained nominally in charge in west Asia while others wielded actual power. As a result, political cracks spiderwebbed across the region, mitigated only in part by shared cultural and economic interests. Then a new group entered the Anatolian peninsula: the Ghuzz (or Oghuz) Turks, a militarily-adept nomadic people from central Asia who had converted to Sunni Islam and adopted many cultural customs from the Persians. They were not

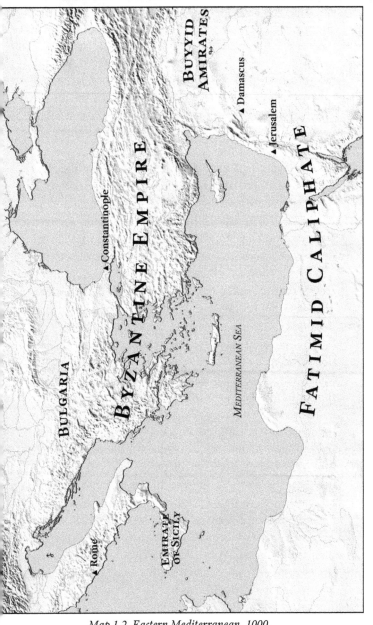

Map 1.2. Eastern Mediterranean, 1000.

a centrally unified people: some groups entered Anatolia when invited to fight for local claimants to power while others came to fulfill their own ambitions. By the middle of the eleventh century, 'Abbasid caliphs in western Asia were figureheads under the control of one Turkic family dynasty, known as the Great Saljuqs.

Although the Great Saljuqs proclaimed that they had ushered in a new Islamic empire, in reality west Asia in the late eleventh century was still politically fractured. In particular, the northeastern Mediterranean and Anatolia formed a principality, the Sultanate of Rum, under the control of mostly independent Saljuq leadership in the late 1070s. Thus, over the course of the eleventh century, west Asia had shifted hands and divided. The Anatolian peninsula and northeastern Mediterranean, in particular, became a frontier zone of sorts, contested by many.

The political situation in west Asia was further destabilized in the late eleventh century. In 1092, Malikshah, a Great Saljuq sultan who had helped stabilize the region, died; he was predeceased by his vizier and chief administrator. Other members of Malikshah's household followed suit in rapid succession. Just two years later, in 1094, the admittedly figurehead 'Abbasid caliph al-Muqtadi died. Succession disputes followed all these deaths. As a result, at the end of the eleventh century, local rulers were thrust back on their own devices and defenses even more than before on the frontiers of the northeastern Mediterranean. In many cases, local rulers disagreed with each other over which faction to support, so were wary of their neighbors. This was the context into which the First Crusade marched.

Moving counterclockwise around the Mediterranean, to the west of Anatolia was the Byzantine Empire (Byzantium), which endured its own political and territorial upheavals in the eleventh century. With its capital Constantinople anchored in the northeast corner of the Mediterranean, Byzantium represented the continuation and evolution of what had been the eastern Roman Empire. Indeed, the Byzantines fully considered themselves Roman. In the words of historian Jonathan Harris, because they saw themselves as the living heirs of the Christian Roman Empire, they believed that "Constantinople occupied a supreme place in the Christian world, over and above Rome or Jerusalem."[8]

In the mid-eleventh century the Byzantine Empire was prosperous, wealthy, and powerful, poised on the intersection of numerous trade routes and fluently engaged with many different regional powers. It shared some cultural characteristics with western European polities, such as Christianity, though sectarian differences between Latin and Byzantine Christianity made that a cause for friction as much as common ground. Byzantium, particularly Constantinople, also shared characteristics with polities in the Islamicate world, such as sophisticated urban living, a professional bureaucratic elite, and a coin-based economy. In pursuit of its own interests, the Byzantine Empire alternately entered into alliances with or waged war against Christian, Muslim, and pagan neighbors. While the empire's main holdings centered

8   Jonathan Harris, *Byzantium and the Crusades*, 2nd ed. (London: Bloomsbury, 2014), 17.

on its capital, emperors also claimed more peripheral lands, including a shrinking assortment of territories in southern Italy.

But the boundaries of the Byzantine Empire were challenged from multiple directions in the later eleventh century. In 1071 the Byzantines found themselves pushed out of Italy altogether by the Normans—originally "north men" from Scandinavia who invaded and then settled in northern France in the tenth century—and a few short years later they faced further Norman aggression much closer to home, in the Balkans. Only the accession of a formidable new Byzantine dynasty in 1081, the Komnenian family led by Emperor Alexios I, put a temporary halt to Norman advances in the Balkans. Alexios had no time to celebrate this pause in the fighting, however. While focused on the Norman threat, the Byzantines had lost most of the territory they claimed in the Anatolian peninsula and the eastern Mediterranean to the Sultanate of Rum. Thus at the end of the eleventh century, Byzantium continued to face threats on eastern and western borders as well as internal rivals for the imperial throne.

Moving to the southern Mediterranean, by 1000 the Shi'ite Fatimid Caliphate controlled north Africa, Sicily, and Egypt, including vital trade routes up the Red Sea from the Indian Ocean. By the 1060s, however, the Fatimids were concentrating on maintaining their central territories in Egypt—all too aware of the sectarian and military threat posed by their Sunni Saljuq neighbors—and thus they allowed other regions to slip from their control. In north Africa, the Fatimids were supplanted by

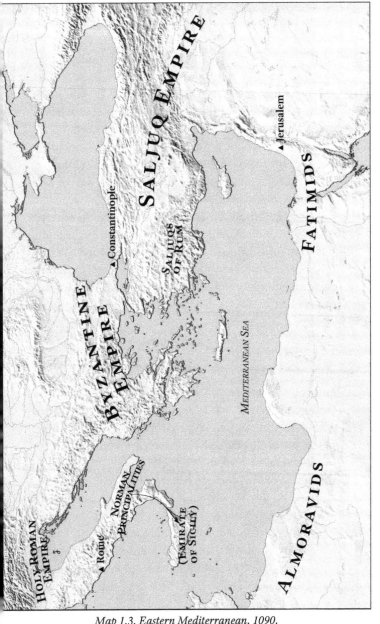

Map 1.3. Eastern Mediterranean, 1090.

their former governors while in Sicily, several independent dynasties came into power. Then, like the Great Saljuqs, the Fatimids were seriously destabilized in the 1090s. In 1094, the Fatimid caliph and his chief military leader died, leading to internal disputes over leadership. In summary, the political situation in the eastern half of the Mediterranean was in flux in the late eleventh century.

At the same time the political situation in the western half was equally complex and equally available for further military opportunism. Since the early eighth century, most of the Iberian peninsula had been ruled by the Sunni Caliphate of Cordoba. This caliphate governed a multi-religious, multi-ethnic population. A few small Christian-ruled kingdoms were located in the mountainous north of the peninsula. They periodically fought both each other and the caliphate.

Then, in 1031, following on the heels of civil war, the Caliphate of Cordoba broke into smaller independent principalities known as *ta'ifa* ("party" or "faction") kingdoms. These *ta'ifa* kingdoms maintained a dynamic and pluralistic cultural milieu, and politically, they vied with each other as well as with Christian-ruled kingdoms in the north. It gradually became common practice for *ta'ifa* kingdoms to deliver tribute (funds and slaves) to the northern kingdoms in return for military assistance. Unsurprisingly, this encouraged the northern kingdoms to view the south as a lucrative prize.

As the eleventh century continued to unfold, the Iberian peninsula witnessed continued political fragmentation and multiple conflicts colored with religious overtones. By the mid-eleventh century, ambitious rulers in the north of

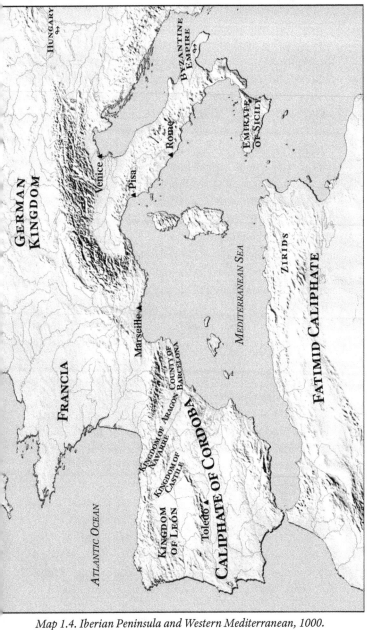

Map 1.4. Iberian Peninsula and Western Mediterranean, 1000.

the peninsula had been joined by often religiously zealous fighters and Latin Christian clerics from what is now France. In 1085, the centrally-located *ta'ifa* city of Toledo was conquered by Alfonso VI, King of Léon-Castile and Galicia. All concerned saw this as a fatal blow to Muslim rule in the peninsula. In fact, however, Alfonso's conquest of Toledo simply prompted new political actors to conquer portions of southern Iberia: the Almoravids. The Almoravids were a highly-motivated Sunni Berber dynasty based in North Africa. They viewed the northern kingdoms as enemies and the *ta'ifa* kingdoms as weak and morally bankrupt. (The *ta'ifa* kings, for their part, considered the Almoravids distinctly uncivilized, though helpful when dealing with encroachment from the north.) Thus, over the course of the eleventh century, the Iberian peninsula went from being mostly unified in terms of government and culture to being heavily fractured and actively contested by variously-motivated armed actors. This resembled the contemporary situation in Anatolia and the eastern Mediterranean, as already described.

Both the territorially-ambitious rulers in north Iberia and the Normans, who were challenging the Byzantine Empire and various Islamicate polities at roughly the same time, can be seen as the vanguard of an energetic Europe in the eleventh century. Yet this was not a united Europe. Indeed, in the eleventh century European political actors competed with each other, and made alliances with extra-European powers, at a fair clip. Modern nation-states as we know them did not exist, and so major political actors included many different—often competing—kings, emperors, and popes, as well as dukes, princes, and

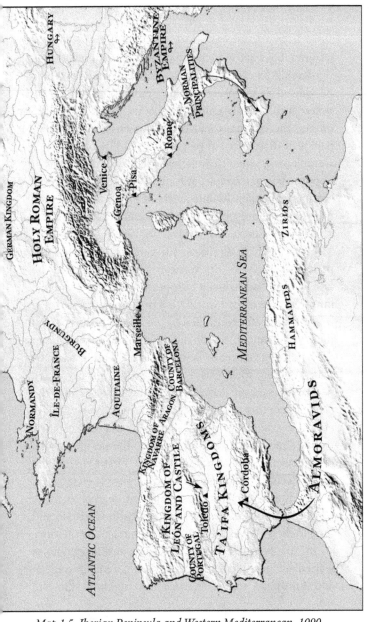

Map 1.5. Iberian Peninsula and Western Mediterranean, 1090.

city-republics like Venice and Genoa. Titles, powers, and borders alike were fluid. The Normans in particular should be viewed as a loosely affiliated ethnic and kin group, rather than a firmly unified people or polity. Like many others, the Normans had their eyes on many different pieces of the territorial pie, and, again like others, they weren't picky about the religious identity of their allies or opponents. For example, at roughly the same time as the Normans attacked Islamic rulers of Sicily, they attacked the last remaining outposts of Byzantium in Italy.

Clearly Europeans were not strangers in the Mediterranean in the eleventh century. Although the political collapse of the western Roman Empire in the fifth century had reduced European engagement and role in the Mediterranean world for a time, nonetheless trade had resumed and continued to link western Europe and the Mediterranean. So too did politics. Meanwhile, Latin Christian pilgrimages by land and sea were undertaken by many different social classes, century after century.

Having said all that, it is nonetheless clear that the eleventh century marked a change. Whether we consider efforts by northern kingdoms in Iberia to, in their words, "reconquer" portions of the Iberian peninsula, the Norman conquest of Sicily, or the First Crusade, the eleventh century witnessed European powers engaging in the Mediterranean world to a different degree. Virtually all of these powers self-identified as Latin Christian and framed their expansionary efforts with religious rhetoric.

In the broadest terms, these expansionary efforts were made possible by the coincidence of Mediterranean and European trends. As just described, in the late eleventh-century Mediterranean there were clear opportunities for expansion made possible by political fragmentation, challenge, and change. At the same time, an uptick in prosperity also enabled growth and expansion in Europe. As we will now see, Latin Christian culture supported this expansion via cultural trends related to the relationship between religion, power, and violence.

The eleventh century saw the beginning of substantial growth in European prosperity. At the most basic level, this was enabled by a distinct climatic trend, the Medieval Climatic Anomaly (MCA). From roughly 950 to 1250, the MCA affected different regions of the world in different ways: some places grew warmer, some cooler, some wetter, some drier. To Europe, the MCA delivered relatively warmer temperatures and greater climatic stability. This warmer and more stable climate, combined with various technological advances—some generated within Europe and others acquired via the Islamicate world—would ultimately lead to higher agricultural yields and safer sea travel. These trends in turn drove population growth, higher standards of living, longer life expectancy, nascent mercantile economies, and a whole host of related cultural developments within Europe.

This growth in prosperity was visible throughout Europe, but most importantly for our purposes, it revitalized northwestern Mediterranean port cities. In the eleventh century, these Latin Christian-ruled urban centers—Genoa, Venice, Naples, Marseilles—increasingly tapped into preexisting trade routes crisscrossing the Mediterranean. Like other trade ports around the Mediterranean, they welcomed small groups from other cultures, regions, and religions to settle and establish long-term neighborhoods in their cities in order to promote trade. Most Mediterranean cities had long been multiethnic and multireligious, regardless of their rulers' religion, so this was a boost to a preexisting trend, rather than a new phenomenon.

What was rather newer was the settlement of Jews in northwestern Europe. Alternately attracted by the economic growth and related opportunities unfolding in the region or deliberately recruited by authorities keen to strategically benefit from their experience with Mediterranean markets and trading practices, small Jewish communities were established in what are now France, England, and Germany in the tenth and eleventh centuries. As Brian Catlos has so conclusively demonstrated, Muslim communities also lived within Latin Christendom and Europe specifically.[9] Thus in the eleventh century religious diversity not only existed around the Mediterranean coast but also within northern Europe.

Prosperity was not the only thing trending upwards in eleventh-century Europe. Piety, too, was increasingly a public and popular concern. In the tenth and eleventh centuries, Latin Christians at many different levels of society demonstrated, and increasingly vocalized, concerns about the state of their souls and the state of Christendom in general. At the risk of oversimplification,

9   Brian A. Catlos, *Muslims of Medieval Latin Christendom, c. 1050–1614* (Cambridge: Cambridge University Press, 2014).

the eleventh century, like others before it, was an age of piety for Latin Christians—and an age of religious reform.

What needed reform and why? One family of concerns centered on the way monasteries functioned. Monasteries were the spiritual engine of Latin Christendom at the time. Monks and nuns prayed for the souls of those departed and for the well-being of Christendom. They were the *milites Christi* ("soldiers of Christ") at the front lines of spiritual combat, fighting the good fight against sin and the forces of evil, acquiring individual spiritual merit, and uplifting their societies along with themselves. Monasteries depended on the social elite—the nobility—who founded, funded, staffed, and protected them.

The cozy relationship between the nobility and the monasteries, as well as some frankly scandalous misbehavior in papal Rome, led to discontent. Critics of the church complained, no doubt sometimes with cause, about simony (the buying and selling of church offices), nepotism, a lack of clerical chastity, an unseemly focus on the acquisition of material wealth, and a purported lack of even the most basic ecclesiastical education. The effectiveness of monastic prayers and the sacraments—and, thus, implicitly, the fate of one's soul—depended upon the genuine virtue and sacred efficacy of the priests and monks in question.

Another family of concerns focused on societal violence. Violence in Latin Christian culture was not new and it was not de facto "unchristian," as already outlined. However, the fact that Christian violence could be justified and charitable—that at its most extreme, Christian holy war was possible—did not mean that

Christian violence was necessarily free from sin. Justice alone did not necessarily make violence a moral good, and so penance—an act that demonstrated contrition and repaid God for sins committed—might be required after performing just violence. Although the idea of Christian violence was well established, beginning in the tenth century many voiced concerns about the details of violence within society—who was violent, when, why, and against whom. The Latin Christian nobility, whose social role hinged upon the performance of violence, were implicated in these concerns.

This dual focus on piety and violence encouraged two related socio-religious movements starting in the mid-tenth century. First, the Peace of God movement tried to limit who could be targeted with violence. Women, children, the poor, and church buildings and personnel should be off limits. Second, the Truce of God movement tried to limit when violence could be appropriately used; Sundays, holy days, and the like were thought inappropriate. Both movements were enthusiastically supported by members of the church and the lower levels of society.

That said, the success of both movements relied upon vows (sacred promises) taken by members of the elite fighting classes. Furthermore, both movements were enforced by means of punitive violence inflicted by vow-keepers upon vow-breakers. So, the goal of these movements was not to end violence or defang the Latin Christian nobility, but rather to direct violence and the elites who performed it. Additionally, the means by which this goal was to be achieved explicitly reinforced the idea of two kinds of violence: "right and good" Christian violence (performed in the right circumstances and by the right people) served to correct immoral, wrongful violence (performed in the wrong circumstances or by the wrong people).

Ultimately reformers interpreted concerns about both ecclesiastical piety and violence as the result of undue lay influences on the Latin church. In other words, from the reformers' perspective, relationships between members of the ecclesiastical hierarchy and lay elites corrupted monasteries and the church in general. The prevalence of immoral, unchristian violence was likewise thought to be caused by out-of-control lay elites. If this was the problem, then the answer seemed clear to reformers inside the Latin church: the church should not rely upon the laity for wealth, power, or authority. In the eleventh century such reformers gradually ascended the steps of power within the Latin church and eventually took the highest seat, that of the pope. From that vantage point, the problem looked less about the relationship between any given noble family and their local church or monastery and more about the relationship between popes and kings, and popes and emperors (i.e., Germanic kings who had been subsequently acclaimed emperor by the papacy).

A certain tension between popes and lay monarchs was hardly new. Since Christendom had long been conceived as a political, social, and cultural entity united in a theocracy, the question of who was at the very top of the power hierarchy was always present. Nonetheless, relative equilibrium between popes and kings/emperors was disrupted dramatically by the eleventh-century reform movement, which sought to ensure the church's independence from lay influence. At the very highest level, this meant that popes should be independent and should guide and be depended upon by secular elites. Popes should trump emperors and kings.

Even if this was a purely theoretical claim, it's easy to see how it might have upset a king or an emperor. However, the matter was not just theoretical; the issue had teeth. In a document usually ascribed to Pope Gregory VII and dated to 1075, the papacy claimed—as the only universal power in the world founded by God alone—the right to depose bishops, to absolve subjects from vows of fealty, to be judged by no other human individual or office, and even to depose emperors. Gregory VII made such claims from a comfortable position, since he enjoyed the ideological and military support of the powerful Countess Matilda of Tuscany.

The emperor at the time, Henry IV of Germany, immediately saw the threat encapsulated in these claims. He was actually not unsympathetic to the goals of the reformers. After all, his father, Henry III, had nominated a reformer to the papacy. But Henry IV could not tolerate the extent of these papal claims. He, like his predecessors, relied upon the right to place clergy into powerful positions, such as bishoprics. Bishops wielded secular as well as spiritual power. Loyal bishops helped counterbalance centrifugal pressures on royal and imperial power generated by powerful German noble families. These papal claims meant that Henry IV would have to contend not only with restless nobles, but also with a group of bishops loyal first and foremost to the pope, whose lands were likewise under papal, not imperial, authority. From Henry's perspective, if he accepted these claims, he would be unable to maintain power without complete submission to the papacy, which he was unwilling to make. Unsurprisingly, then, Henry IV's response was to issue firm counterclaims: Gregory VII was, in Henry's view, a false and impious individual who should be deposed from the papal seat.

Thus began a decades-long conflict between Latin Christian emperors and popes. Historians call this the Investiture Conflict, because debate often focused on the question of who should invest bishops with their bishoprics and lands. On both sides this conflict was waged with words, political actions (including the elevation of alternative anti-emperors and anti-popes), and military force. This particular conflict would not be resolved until 1122, while the larger issue of papal-imperial (or papal-regnal) relations would surface repeatedly all through the medieval and early modern period.

There are three reasons why this conflict matters for the history of the crusades. First, the First Crusade was launched in the midst of the Investiture Conflict. As discussed more fully in the next chapter, the pope who launched it was contending with an imperial anti-pope who had control of the city of Rome at the time. Thus the crusade should be read in the context of papal-imperial politics; it was a significant move in that internecine conflict.

Second, papal claims to military force became ever more explicit and pervasive before and during the

Investiture Conflict. Papal claims to legitimate use of military force were not new, but reform popes had deliberately stepped up and intensified these claims. For example, in 1053 Pope Leo IX personally led armies against Norman forces in southern Italy, in 1063 Pope Alexander II granted a collective spiritual reward to those who would fight against one of his enemies, and in 1074 Gregory VII called upon all Latin Christians to aid the Byzantines by fighting against the Saljuqs. Subsequently Gregory claimed the authority to call Christians to arms to defend the cause of the church and himself as pope (he considered these causes identical) against Henry IV and his allies.

Third, the conflict—and the various claims and issues that arose during it—affected and reflected dynamics in the Mediterranean more broadly. The Investiture Conflict was not only an internecine Latin Christian affair. After all, the papacy had long been a political actor in the Mediterranean because it ruled its own lands in Italy. These lands were bordered variously by Byzantine outposts, German imperial holdings in northern Italy, and locales (like Sicily) governed at times by Islamic powers.

In the eleventh century popes sought allies among all these various powers in order to defend or expand papal lands. These alliances were, to say the least, flexible. Take, for example, relations between the Normans and Leo IX. As just noted, in 1053 Leo allied with the Byzantines and led armies against Norman forces in southern Italy—unsuccessfully. He was then held captive by the Normans until he acknowledged the Norman conquests as legitimate. Leo was thus at best a lukewarm friend to the Normans. Yet much the same could be said about his relations with the Byzantines. Although his armies fought on their side in 1053, he also directly contributed to a major schism between the Latin and Byzantine churches.

We see similar adroit maneuvers during the papal reign of Gregory VII. In 1074 Gregory excommunicated Robert Guiscard, the Norman patriarch who, despite previous alliances with the Muslim rulers of Sicily, spearheaded the eventual conquest of the island. In the same year, Gregory VII called upon all Christians to aid the Byzantines against the Saljuqs. These events would seem to place the papacy firmly with the Byzantines and against the Normans. However, the Investiture Conflict and the papacy's need for armed allies to oppose imperial forces shifted the playing field. In 1084 Gregory VII restored good relations with the Normans when Henry IV's armies marched on Rome. In the end, this move backfired spectacularly on Gregory; Norman troops did indeed retake Rome, but they promptly sacked the city. Outraged Roman citizens forced the pope to flee to the Norman-held city of Salerno.

The point is not that the papacy was a more pliable or inconsistent ally than others, but rather, that the Mediterranean in the eleventh century was fluid and vigorous, and that Latin Christian rulers, both lay and ecclesiastical, engaged flexibly in this environment. The First Crusade did not occur in a static world in which unified Christians and unified Muslims faced each other down in a perpetual "us vs. them" struggle. Neither did it occur in a world that believed in Christian (or any other kind of) pacifism. It occurred, instead, in the dynamic and rapidly changing landscape of the eleventh-century Mediterranean, in which Christian and Muslim rulers alternately allied and contended with each other and amongst themselves for political, economic, and religious advantages. All the while the diverse peoples they ruled pursued their own goals, as individuals or as members of regional, religious, or cultural groups. In the more narrowly defined landscape of Europe, Latin Christians were increasingly concerned with piety and increasingly sought to both restrain and deploy violence in the pressing pursuit of salvation.

Further Reading

Abulafia, David. *The Great Sea: A Human History of the Mediterranean*. Reprint. Oxford: Oxford University Press, 2013.

Abu-Lughod, Janet L. *Before European Hegemony: The World System A.D. 1250–1350*. Oxford: Oxford University Press, 1991.

Blumenthal, Uta-Renate. *The Investiture Controversy: Church and Monarchy from the Ninth to the Twelfth Century*. Philadelphia: University of Pennsylvania Press, 1991.

Catlos, Brian A. *Muslims of Medieval Latin Christendom c. 1050–1614*. Cambridge: Cambridge University Press, 2014.

Davis-Secord, Sarah. *Where Three Worlds Met: Sicily in the Early Medieval Mediterranean*. Ithaca NY: Cornell University Press, 2017.

Koch, Bettina. *Patterns Legitimizing Political Violence: Islamic and Christian Traditions and Legacies*. Berlin and Boston: De Gruyter, 2016.

Lamb, Hubert H. *Climate, History, and the Modern World*. 2nd ed. London and New York: Routledge, 1995.

Lapidus, Ira M. *A History of Islamic Societies*. 2nd ed. Cambridge: Cambridge University Press, 2002.

Malegam, Jehangir Yezdi. *The Sleep of Behemoth: Disputing Peace and Violence in Medieval Europe, 1000–1200*. Ithaca NY: Cornell University Press, 2013.

Sizgorich, Thomas. *Violence and Belief in Late Antiquity: Militant Devotion in Christianity and Islam*.

Philadelphia: University of Pennsylvania Press, 2008.

Tellenbach, Gerd. *The Church in Western Europe from the Tenth to the Early Twelfth Century*. Cambridge: Cambridge University Press, 1993.

Treadgold, Warren. *A History of Byzantine State and Society*. Stanford: Stanford University Press, 1997.

II

Constructing the First Crusade: Contexts, Events, and Reactions

AS THE PREVIOUS CHAPTER MADE CLEAR, THE FIRST Crusade did not spring fully formed into an otherwise static world. It was informed by ongoing trends and opportunities, including political fragmentation in the eastern Mediterranean, European prosperity, and cultural trends and political disputes within Latin Christendom. Yet at the same time, the First Crusade was not inevitable. After all, when Pope Urban II preached what would become the First Crusade in 1095, he knew that Gregory VII had also urged Latin Christians to aid the Byzantines against the Saljuqs—and he knew that Gregory's urgings had fallen flat.

As this chapter demonstrates, the First Crusade conquest of Jerusalem in 1099 occurred in and affected a complex Mediterranean world. Furthermore the meanings ascribed to the events of the crusade were several right from the beginning. Writers in Latin Christendom, the Byzantine Empire, and the Islamicate world sought to explain what had happened in different ways. By the middle of the twelfth century, the crusading movement was actively evolving and popular in Latin Christendom. However, the crusade of 1147–49 would demonstrate that the Mediterranean continued to be complex and dynamic; crusade planning and popularity were no substitute for full knowledge of the political landscape.

***

Narratives of the crusades sometimes imagine Urban II travelling triumphantly on the 1095 preaching tour that inspired the First Crusade. The reality was a little less heroic. You'll remember that Gregory VII's papacy ended in shambles in 1085, with the pope excluded from the city of Rome. Gregory's successor, Pope Victor III, who literally tried to run away when informed of his election to the papal see, lasted only a year in office due to ill health. In the meantime, Norman forces continued to fight imperial armies, who in turn rallied around their own proclaimed pope who held Rome until a crusading army delivered it to Urban in 1097. Thus Urban was in fact largely unwelcome in the city of Rome in 1095; he did not launch the First Crusade from a position of unimpeachable papal power.

Indeed, as already emphasized, one context in which to view the First Crusade is that of the papal-imperial contest for ultimate authority within Latin Christendom. Urban's 1095 preaching tour through what is now northern Italy and France was a proactive response to a relatively precarious position. Like any political campaign, Urban's tour served to build and reaffirm relationships with a variety of local powers, both ecclesiastical and lay. It furthermore allowed him to continue advancing reform goals through local and regional church councils, and, especially, to advertise to French bishops a substantial council to be held at Clermont in November 1095. Last but not least, this was the first such tour undertaken by a pope, and so many people at all levels of society had the novel experience of actually seeing a pope in their midst, with the full and deliberate theatricality of Urban's entourage. In this context, Urban's appeal for an armed expedition to the eastern Mediterranean—a call that was deliberately pitched at the Frankish nobility and knights, rather than royal or imperial powers—was a reaffirmation of the papacy's moral supremacy and right to direct and sanctify warfare. It was furthermore a reassertion of Urban's personal status as pope. Given that Urban's appeal was successful, it was also a vivid demonstration of the papacy's ability to inspire warfare, even if some of the events that followed were not necessarily as Urban might have wished.

A second context for understanding the First Crusade is that of Byzantine domestic and foreign relations on the one hand and Norman ambitions on the other. Urban II did not come up with the idea for an armed campaign against the Saljuqs by himself. As we've seen, the idea was first floated by Gregory VII in response to the Byzantine Empire's ongoing battle against Saljuq forces in Anatolia. The Byzantine emperor Alexios I Komnenos had directly appealed for military aid as he worked unceasingly to manage the Normans on his western frontier, the Saljuqs to the east, and political machinations at home in Constantinople. By the late eleventh century, many Norman contingents and other fighting forces from Europe had fought as mercenaries or auxiliaries under Byzantine direction in the eastern Mediterranean. As far as we can determine, in the 1090s Alexios's hope was for a similar kind of armed assistance in regaining lands lost to the Saljuqs.

Thus Alexios was not necessarily a passive actor—as has been assumed in the past—nor was he a hapless figure begging for assistance from a more powerful Latin Christendom. His role in launching the First Crusade was most likely deliberate and considered, even if—as for Urban II—subsequent events did not play out as he had envisioned.[10] In Alexios's case, he surely did not want the same Normans he had just fought in the Balkans to wind up possessing territory in his backyard, and yet they did, as we shall see. For the Normans themselves, many of

---

10 Historians continue to debate the precise role played by Alexios in the launch of the First Crusade. For a recent summary of the debate, see Jonathan Harris, "Byzantium and the First Crusade: Three Avenues of Approach," *Estudios bizantinos* 2 (2014): 125–41. DOI: 10.1344/EBizantinos2014.2.5.

them the same families and individuals who had defeated Islamicate and Byzantine forces in southern Italy, the First Crusade offered another outlet for their territorial ambitions and another way to build upon and benefit from their relationship with the papacy.

Neither context, however, fully explains why Urban II's appeal actually resulted in action. Again, Gregory VII had made a very similar appeal in 1074, yet did not receive the same response. Why did Latin Christians rally to Urban's call for an armed expedition to the eastern Mediterranean? The answer rests in two factors: first, the persuasive combination of ideas brought together and intensified by Urban, and second, the audience to which he appealed.

Like virtually all historical sources, our sources for the ideas Urban used are imperfect. We do not have the text of his sermon exactly as it was delivered; instead, we have later versions and representations of it in medieval chronicles. Of these chronicles, only a few were written by eyewitnesses and all were written after the 1099 conquest of Jerusalem by the crusaders. In addition to these chronicles, we have papal letters and conciliar documents. Arguably all of these sources were affected, to some degree, by the knowledge that the First Crusade ultimately succeeded. Many of the chronicles in particular bear the clear marks of authors with a particular ax or two to grind; none of our surviving accounts of Urban's address were written by pro-imperial authors.

Taken together, these sources reveal a few repeating themes and motifs that seem to have been present in 1095. First, Urban clearly tapped into the preexisting practice of pilgrimage to Jerusalem. Pilgrimages large and small had been a part of Christian devotional practices for centuries. Pilgrimage to Jerusalem was, in many ways, the pilgrimage to end all pilgrimages, both because of Jerusalem's status in the Latin Christian worldview and because of the hardships involved in travelling to Jerusalem from Europe. We see a surge in pilgrimages to Jerusalem in the lead up to the year 1000, in part due to apocalyptic expectations. On the whole, Islamic rulers viewed Christian pilgrims—whether Latin, Byzantine, or other—as a source of revenue, and did not stop them from journeying to Jerusalem. While the number of Latin Christian pilgrimages dropped after damage done to Jerusalem's Holy Sepulcher in 1009 by order of the eccentric Fatimid caliph al-Hakim, throughout the eleventh century the numbers of Latin pilgrims to Jerusalem gradually but fairly steadily increased again. Thus in one sense, the First Crusade was just another, albeit large, armed, and aggressive, group of pilgrims trundling towards Jerusalem.

This particular pilgrimage—the First Crusade—needed to be armed because, Urban claimed, "liberation" was necessary: the liberation of the church and oppressed Christians and the liberation of the holy land. This theme of Christian liberation was not new, to say the least. Most recently it had been used, repeatedly, by the eleventh-century reformers who were discussed in the previous chapter. The Peace of God Movement, the Truce of God Movement, and the full-fledged reform movement embodied by popes like Leo IX and Gregory VII all made use of the rhetoric of liberation. This liberation was to be achieved by force; remember that the Peace and Truce of

God were enforced through violence, and reform popes had legitimated the use of force against imperial and anti-reform individuals. So, in many ways Latin Christendom was well primed to harken to the call to liberate the church by means of violence.

Given all this, nonetheless, taking part in an armed expedition thousands of miles away was obviously a risky undertaking for many different reasons. One was likely to suffer or die on the way and one's family and property would be at risk. Why would anyone commit to do this? The post-1099 narrative accounts of Urban's sermon present us with a veritable buffet of reasons, but there is one reason that shines through most clearly in those accounts and in papal letters and conciliar documents: because this was an opportunity to move closer to eternal salvation; because this warfare would be penitential and divinely directed, and thus spiritually beneficial.

These ideas were not entirely brand new. Once again, the ideological roots lay in the papal-imperial conflict. Earlier in the eleventh century, a group of thinkers supported by Matilda of Tuscany provided justification for Gregory's assertions that fighting in a just cause could constitute penance because of the danger and hardship involved. Centuries before then, other popes had made claims about the spiritual benefits to be had by fighting on behalf of the Latin Christian church.

But although the development of penitential violence and penitential warfare can be seen well before 1095, the combination of the ideas and practices of penitential warfare, Christian liberation, and Jerusalem pilgrimage was unusually heady. The spiritual benefits on offer for the First Crusade were, arguably, unprecedented—or at least, unprecedentedly appealing to their audience. It had become possible to envision and perform violence that was not only justified and charitable, but a positive moral good in the eyes of the pope himself. It had become possible to engage in a violent enterprise that, instead of requiring even the smallest amount of penance, was itself spiritually cleansing, i.e., penitential. The virtual violence engaged in for centuries in the spiritual war against evil by Christian monastics, the original *milites Christi*, was now joined by physical violence performed by the laity, the new *milites Christi*.

Crucially, these ideas were delivered to a highly receptive audience. Indeed, "highly receptive audience" may be an understatement. The earliest surviving narrative account of the First Crusade, the *Gesta Francorum* ("Deeds of the Franks"), actually describes a popular religious movement sweeping Frankish lands *first*, and the papacy cashing in on it *later*. As outlined in the previous chapter, Latin Christians were already concerned about salvation and about violence. They were already actively trying to find a way for the fighting nobility to live as Christians and already employing Christian violence in pursuit of that goal. The First Crusade offered this audience a way to move decisively towards salvation while continuing to perform the acts of violence they were socialized to do.

It would be a mistake, however, to imagine that the crusaders were nothing but neat ranks of noble men and their armed households. The papacy sought to recruit trained armed men and exclude others, but—and not for the last time—the papacy was unable to fully control the expedition once launched. Virtually all elements of Latin Christian society were mobilized—men and women, young and old, the powerful and the poor, lay people and churchmen, those who regularly fought and those who had never done so. Mind you, the breadth of backgrounds among crusaders should not be taken to mean that in quantitative terms most people in Europe went on crusade; the vast majority of Latin Christians declined the very real dangers and expenses of the expedition. Nonetheless, the challenge of handling large groups of people with widely varying degrees of experience and resources had become and would remain central in the crusading movement.

Urban's preaching was amplified by other preachers around Europe in the weeks and months that followed his sermon at Clermont. The news furthermore spread by word of mouth, particularly within families and social networks; both men and women influenced their loved ones and associates to crusade. Those intending to participate took vows and placed crosses on their outer garments. As a result, the first crusaders were on the move in 1096, though the First Crusade was not a once and done movement. In fact, it can be divided into at least three successive waves of movement, all of which took the land route to Jerusalem via Constantinople. The first, impetuous wave departed in spring 1096, the second wave headed off in August 1096, per papal directions, and the third wave got underway in 1099, inspired by news of the conquest of Jerusalem. Even after 1100, individual crusaders and small groups would continue to grab arms and go east on a more ad hoc basis.

The people and events of the second wave became embedded in medieval and modern memory as "the first" crusade. Yet the second wave itself comprised many different households, families, and individuals, and second wave contingents moved independently of each other. There was no single military leader of the second wave or of the crusade as a whole. Instead, a number of powerful nobles provided collective leadership, alternately cooperating and competing with each other. Both the cooperation and the competition were surely boosted by the fact that a number of these nobles were linked by familial as well as political relationships. Despite the tensions generated by these relationships, the second wave of the First Crusade was, from the Latin Christian perspective, successful, and because the First Crusade quickly became and continues to serve as a prototype expedition in popular memory, it is worth reviewing its key events.

The Latins' fight against perceived enemies of Christendom began while they were still in Europe and their first casualties were European Jews—first in France, just after the Council of Clermont, and then in the Rhineland, in what is now Germany, as crusaders got underway in May 1096. In community after community, Jewish people were alternately killed, offered the chance to convert, or forcibly baptized. Their material assets were seized, and many chose to kill themselves and their loved ones rather than convert.

Assessing the forces behind the massacres of 1096 is complicated, but it seems indisputable that for some there

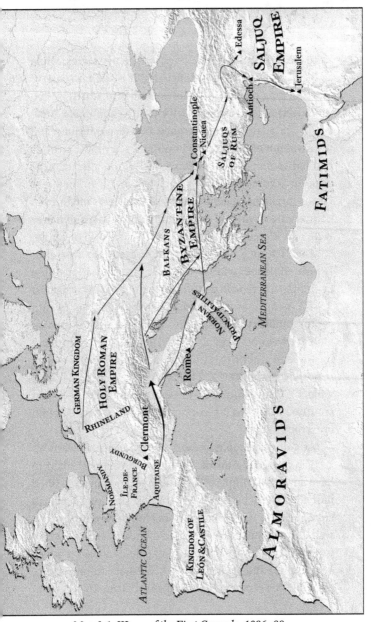

Map 2.1. Waves of the First Crusade, 1096–99.

were clear economic incentives for the massacres, while at the same time, others concluded it made no sense to march a long distance to fight "enemies of Christ" when there were said enemies much closer to home. For some Latin Christians, the difference between Muslims and Jews was not of the greatest importance; a similar attitude had led to anti-Jewish violence in Europe after damage done to Jerusalem's Holy Sepulcher in 1009. For other Latin Christians, the evidence suggests, Jews might even be more deserving of violence than Muslims, since they were considered responsible for the crucifixion of Christ.

The 1096 massacres do not constitute the first anti-Jewish violence within Europe, but they signal the beginning of repeated and escalating violence against Jewish people and communities through the twelfth century and beyond. They also remind us that crusading violence was not—arguably could not be—fully controlled by any one authority, not even in 1096. The papacy and many lay authorities explicitly condemned anti-Jewish violence before and after 1096, yet such violence would continue, and would continue to be associated with crusading.

At Constantinople in late 1096, the second wave hit a sticking point. Alexios I was by no means thrilled to have massive groups of both armed and impoverished individuals—including many of his previous Norman adversaries in the Balkans—knocking up against his city walls. The Latins had maintained themselves on the trip to Constantinople through pillaging (the common practice at the time) and their claims to "be there to help" were heard with a certain amount of skepticism. The fact that

Alexios's rule was disputed by various Byzantine factions made the situation even riskier for him.

From his perspective, Alexios managed the situation using traditional Byzantine diplomatic strategies. First he isolated the various leaders of the second wave. Then, in return for gifts and funds—which served to buy supplies from Byzantine markets and demonstrate the incredible wealth of the empire—Alexios asked each leader for two oaths made according to their own customs. First, the Latins were to return to the Byzantine Empire any lands they captured that had once belonged to it, and second, they were to swear homage and fealty to Alexios. The Latin leaders were unhappy with this request but their options were limited, and ultimately almost all grudgingly swore the oaths in order to move forward. Whether they or Alexios would keep their oaths would remain to be seen.

Across the Bosporus and marching towards Nicaea, the second wave experienced two rude awakenings. First, they kept tripping over the bones of the first wave, whose most successful groups had barely made it farther than Nicaea before disintegrating under the pressure of incompetence, foolhardiness, and highly effective Saljuq assaults. Second, the crusaders found that they were unable to take the city of Nicaea by themselves. Nicaea, the strongly fortified seat of the Saljuq Sultan of Rum, Qilij Arslan, ultimately surrendered after negotiation to Alexios and the Byzantines. The Latins woke up on the day they intended to assault Nicaea to find imperial flags flying and themselves barred from entering the city.

Depending on one's perspective, this may have looked like teamwork or treachery.

You may wonder why Nicaea surrendered at all, since it was so strongly fortified. The reason for the surrender of Nicaea—and ultimately one of the most convincing reasons for the Latin Christian conquest of Jerusalem—rests in the complex and unstable political situation in Anatolia and the eastern Mediterranean in the 1090s, as outlined in Chapter 1. Due to this instability, which put immense pressure on local leaders in the region, Qilij Arslan, the Sultan of Rum, was away from Nicaea with his armies when the Latins showed up. The Latins and Byzantines benefitted from a regional political situation they had not created nor, at least in the case of the Latins, anticipated.

Despite these setbacks in morale at Nicaea, most but not all participants in the second wave marched to Antioch more or less directly after Nicaea. Two of the second wave's leaders, Tancred and Baldwin of Boulogne, broke away and independently moved through the region, alternately pillaging and making alliances as seemed most advantageous. After all, Anatolia was majority Christian, and some local leaders who were Christians saw the Latin presence as an opportunity to advance their own causes. Most notably, Baldwin of Boulogne managed to establish the first Latin principality in the eastern Mediterranean, centered on the city of Edessa. For the rest of the second wave, the journey from Nicaea to Antioch lasted for approximately four tortuous months. The main problem was not starvation—yet—but rather the toll that the heat took on horses and pack animals. By the time the main group reached Antioch, many knights were horseless. This inconvenienced, incapacitated, and dishonored those accustomed to fighting on horseback.

All present in the eastern Mediterranean recognized the city of Antioch's religious, economic, and political importance. Thus despite the political fragility of the Islamicate world at that moment, a coalition of forces rallied to march to Antioch and oppose the Latins there. They rightly foresaw that events at Antioch itself would prove pivotal for the second wave. The Latins carried on a seven-and-a-half-month siege of the city through the winter, in a region quickly stripped of food, which was excruciating on both sides of the city walls. Latin leaders disagreed about how to take the city. In the end, Bohemond of Taranto convinced his peers to promise to give him the city if Alexios I didn't come claim it and Bohemond's troops were first over the walls. When all had agreed, Bohemond then revealed that he had already convinced a citizen of Antioch to betray the city.

Yet all too quickly, the Latins were themselves besieged in Antioch by Kerbogha, the governor of Mosul and leader of the aforesaid Islamicate coalition. The city's resources had already been fully depleted and the Latins faced starvation and despair. In this impossible position, some deserted, most famously Count Stephen of Blois. The Byzantines did not send aid, in part because Alexios heard from Stephen on his flight westward. Based on what Stephen reported, Alexios considered Antioch effectively lost and moved his armies back towards Constantinople. This seemed like wise prudence to the Byzantines and bald faithlessness to most of the Latins. Meanwhile, in the city, Latin leaders disagreed about what to do. Soon, they also disagreed about whether the Holy Lance—the lance purportedly used to strike Jesus's side while on the cross—had actually been miraculously found thanks to divine visions, or whether its revelation was a deceit designed to tip popular opinion towards one Latin leader or another.

Facing death by starvation, the outnumbered Latins marched out to meet Kerbogha and were, surprisingly, victorious. Many later claimed divine and saintly assistance on the battlefield, though historians readily point to the fragile unity of the coalition forces opposing the Latins, a unity that clearly could not withstand pitched battle. As it turned out, members of the Islamicate coalition were not the only ones struggling with fragile unity. After the Battle of Antioch, the Latin leaders of the second wave fractured more decisively; relations with Alexios and disagreements about when to move to Jerusalem affected the fault lines. Lacking full consensus, Latin forces spread out and took a city here and a city there. Fear of the Latins had by now become widespread, and sources tell us of savage practices of war, including cannibalism. Faced with these reports and knowing they had only their own resources to rely upon, many local rulers, Muslim and Christian alike, offered tribute to the Latins if they would only remain at a distance.

This situation was unlikely to prompt the second wave to quickly move on and lose more tribute. However, not everyone was primarily concerned with acquisition. Ultimately the lower social classes forced the question of when to proceed to Jerusalem in fulfillment of their vows.

Most of the second wave moved to take Jerusalem in early spring 1099, though some did not accompany them, notably Bohemond, now Prince of Antioch, and Baldwin, now Count of Edessa. At that point in time, Jerusalem had changed hands three times in the last 30 years alone: the city was occupied violently by an ambitious Turkoman in the 1070s; claimed by the Saljuqs and given to a Saljuq *amir* ("commander") in 1079; and violently taken by the Fatimids in 1098, less than a year before the crusader armies arrived. One can only imagine the gloom felt by the city's inhabitants at the sight of yet more army encampments.

The Latin siege of Jerusalem began in early June 1099. The Latins knew that Fatimid armies were on the way and moved quickly: on July 15 the siege ended in conquest of the city and massacre of many of its inhabitants, who were Muslims, Jews, and Christians. While it is difficult to get an exact picture of the violence and death, in part because Latin sources positively exulted in the bloodshed while Arabic sources differed in their treatment of the event, it seems clear that nonetheless many died. Though Jerusalem was the stated goal of the crusade, the Battle of Jerusalem was not the final major armed conflict engaged in by the second wave; that was the Battle of Ascalon in early August 1099. Despite the grandiose claims of Latin Christian chronicles of the First Crusade, most historians agree that the primary and decisive factor that enabled the Latin conquest of Jerusalem was political turmoil in the Islamicate eastern Mediterranean and Anatolia in the 1090s.

In the aftermath of the Latin conquest of Jerusalem, communities around the Mediterranean struggled to adjust to a new political reality. Godfrey of Bouillon had been chosen to rule a new Latin Kingdom of Jerusalem, one of four Latin-ruled polities in the eastern Mediterranean that were conquered and created in the early twelfth century. In the aggregate, historians often refer to these polities as the "crusader states." Clearly, the political map had shifted for all Mediterranean actors and specific relationships would have to be felt out and established. As we will see, alliances would not be clear-cut, fixed, or made predictably along religious fault lines. Furthermore, internal politics within the crusader states and between them and the rest of Latin Christendom also had to be sorted out, not least in terms of the ongoing papal-imperial conflict. For whom, exactly, was the conquest of Jerusalem a victory?

Yet another part of this adjustment was to ponder the new reality and provide an explanation for it. What had just happened and why? As ever, the answers depended upon whom one asked, though it is worth noting that all perspectives agreed on one thing: the material world reflected divine will. Thus, to a greater or lesser extent, and with different implications, all parties considered the Latin conquests to be an expression of God's will.

For the most part, Islamic historians and commentators did not view the Latin expedition in the eastern Mediterranean as "new" or the "first" of anything. Many in the late eleventh century simply expressed confusion and alarm about what had happened. Those who did attempt to explain events placed them firmly within the context

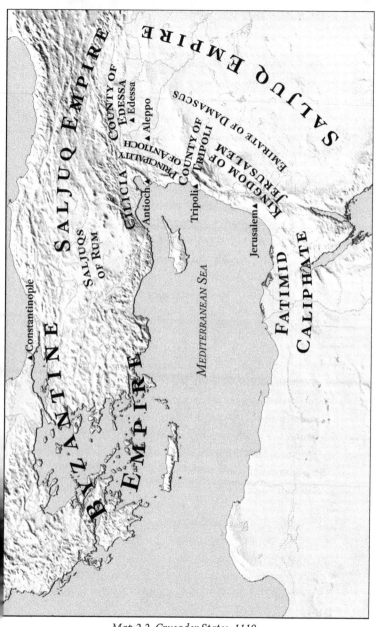

Map 2.2. Crusader States, 1110.

of eleventh-century Latin expansion in Iberia and Sicily. In the late eleventh century, only a minority interpreted the crusaders as religiously motivated, though that would change in the twelfth century, as we'll see.

Jewish writers around the Mediterranean also placed the crusade into a previously-established and longstanding history: that of Jewish martyrdom. As before in Jewish history, God was testing the Jewish people's faith and punishing their sins. The Latins were thus divine instruments and the cause of their actions was divine will. Within Europe, Jewish accounts—written in Hebrew for Jewish audiences—sought to explicitly commemorate the active martyrdom of Jewish people in the Rhineland. These accounts ascribe a variety of motivations to the Latins, ranging from a desire for righteous vengeance to simple greed, but explaining the crusaders was not a priority; rather, these texts sought to commemorate and celebrate those who had died. More fragmentary sources from Jewish people in the eastern Mediterranean who were wealthy enough to flee the crusade describe disrupted families as well as material want and the challenges of captivity.

Byzantine historians, most notably Alexios's daughter, Anna Komnene, who wrote in the mid-twelfth century, positioned the events of 1096–99 within Byzantine imperial history. She too, if only by the way she organized her account, connected the expedition to earlier Norman-Byzantine conflicts in the Balkans. Furthermore, from her perspective, things weren't "done" or "over"; related events were still unspooling for Byzantium. Post-1099 Bohemond and the Byzantines (aided by the Venetians) were actively at war with each other until Bohemond finally submitted to Alexios in 1108. Even after that, the Byzantines had to deal with their new neighbors, the crusader states. In her account of events, Anna Komnene marveled at the Latins, at times admiring their military skill, ferocity, and religious commitment, while at other moments denigrating what she considered unsophisticated religious zealotry, Germanic barbarity, and unseemly ambition. She distinguished among the leaders of the second wave, clearly (and correctly) representing Normans such as Bohemond as a threat to the empire.

In the early to mid-twelfth century, Latin Christian enthusiasts quickly and deliberately established the First Crusade—referred to as a "journey," "pilgrimage," "expedition," or "business of Christ"—as a new cultural benchmark within the history of (Latin) Christendom. Ecclesiastical authors produced a flurry of accounts commemorating the events of 1096–99. These texts did not simply record events. In many ways they created them, by placing them in a framework of interpretation that would prove remarkably durable through the centuries that followed. These accounts suggested a range of precedents for the events of 1096–99. These precedents were primarily biblical, but others fell into categories we today would consider historical or mythological: the exploits of classical heroes; the Maccabees; the destruction of Jerusalem by Titus and Vespasian in 70 CE; Charlemagne's conquests in the seventh and eighth centuries. Nonetheless, it was stressed repeatedly, the events of 1096–99 were in some way unprecedented and the first of a new kind. Clearly, this historical interpretation has remained influential and dominant for many centuries.

These Latin Christian narratives made use of Urban's themes of liberation, pilgrimage, and penitential violence, but added (we suspect) further and varied nuances. The call for liberation was graphically justified with reports of atrocities. Purported outrages had been committed against fellow Christians—"brothers and sisters" in Christ. The holy land, God's land, the land where Christ suffered, "mother Jerusalem" herself, had been reportedly desecrated by "enemies of Christ." It was thus presented as imperative that Christians answer Urban's call for four broad reasons. First, because horrible injuries required Christian vengeance. After all, one had duties as a fighting people who desired to polish up family reputations and not let down the ancestors, and passages from the New Testament supported the righteous vengeance of the godly; some accounts explicitly called out the Franks as a noble people chosen by God, like the Israelites. Second, because crusading was represented in some ways as an act of *imitatio Christi* ("the imitation of Christ"). Crusaders were described carrying their crosses and walking in the footsteps of Christ; they were also described as victorious like Christ. Third, because this might well be the end of days. And with that in mind, fourth—most importantly— because by doing so, one could atone for one's sins (they were numerous), advance towards eternal salvation, and avoid the wrath of a disappointed and justly angered God. In other words, on top of the themes believed to have been present in 1095, Latin Christian writers laid down additional and sympathetic layers of language, symbolism, and meaning in the early twelfth century.

But even within Latin Christendom the meaning of the First Crusade wasn't singular, nor was it created by the Latin church alone. Noble families and individuals in Europe also quickly sought to memorialize the crusading deeds of themselves and their kin on their own terms. Whether in the architecture and decoration of churches and monasteries that they supported, the material goods that they bought, or the family histories that they commissioned, lay men and women built crusading into Latin Christian culture. It even permeated popular culture; composers seized upon the dramatic events of the First Crusade to craft and perform lyric and epic poetry that celebrated Latin Christian triumph. In all these cultural phenomena, we can discern both echoes of form and content that had come before and a sense that something newly substantial had just occurred.

One such "old and new" cultural phenomenon was the concept of a military order. Military orders combined the moral imperatives of other religious orders (like chastity and obedience) with a moral imperative to commit acts of physical violence on behalf of God and the church. The earliest military orders formed in the Kingdom of Jerusalem in the early twelfth century. The order of the Knights of the Temple (or Templars) was founded in Jerusalem in the years after 1099, while the already-established Hospital of St. John (or Hospitallers), added a military role to its original mission as a hospital starting in the 1120s. Both orders—and the idea of military orders in general—were popular, and religious houses for these orders and others were founded in Europe, too. As subsequent chapters will discuss, military orders would have a major impact on crusading history in the centuries to come.

It is hopefully quite clear that crusading did not simply stop after the 1099 Latin conquest of Jerusalem. How could it, given this fertile cultural environment in Latin Christendom, the needs and evolution of the crusader states, and the active responses forming within the Islamicate and Byzantine spheres? The landscape of crusading history is not one of discrete military endeavors standing out in an otherwise uneventful timeline, like single towers scattered sparsely across a vast plain. Instead, crusading history looks more like a forest, with the largest and best remembered expeditions standing tall but surrounded on all sides by other trees of different heights—not to mention bushes and undergrowth.

Thus in the first half of the twelfth century, we see smaller sallies aimed at various Mediterranean targets, including, in 1135, against enemies of the papacy in southern Italy. Sometimes these crusades were purely the result of papal initiative, while often they reflected the initiative of others supported by the papacy; for example, Queens Teresa of Portugal and Urraca of León and Castile continued to wage wars against Muslim opponents that were "declared to be equivalent to crusades" by Pope Paschal II.[11] We also see small groups and individuals

---

11 Helen J. Nicholson, "Women's Involvement in the Crusades," in *The Crusader World*, ed. Adrian J. Boas (London and New York: Routledge, 2016), 54.

simply taking off to fight "enemies of Christ," apparently believing themselves part of a larger and ongoing endeavor. At the same time, unarmed pilgrimage to Jerusalem also continued.

Understanding the growth of crusading within Latin Christendom—in a plurality of forms—is necessary to understand the expedition of 1147–49 (called the Second Crusade by nineteenth-century European historians). The traditional and oversimplified explanation for this major multinational expedition is that a zealous Islamic ruler (Zangi) conquered the city of Edessa in 1144, prompting a panicked and equally zealous Latin Christian response. This traditional explanation falls down when events are set into a broader context, and even more when we consider that the Latin Kingdom of Jerusalem had been asking for more military aid from Europe—either ad hoc or additional major expeditions—all through the early twelfth century, with only limited success.

Why, then, did Zangi's conquest of Edessa spark another massive expedition? To a limited degree, it did signal a revitalized and reunified Islamic presence in the eastern Mediterranean, one that had effectively harnessed the rhetoric of military *jihad* and that posed a greater threat to the crusader states; these dynamics are discussed in greater depth in the following chapter. It's unclear, however, that Latin Christians in Europe recognized this. Thus we have to look to two other factors to explain why the crusade of 1147–49 was successful in rallying support in Europe. First, the city of Edessa was of symbolic importance, since it had been the first crusader state established. Second, and more importantly, crusading ideas and culture had been growing within Latin Christendom, and by 1144, major actors—both royal and papal—were primed to respond.

In the 1140s the Latin church was well positioned, both ideologically and in terms of its leaders, to grab hold of the idea of a substantial crusade and not let go. The pope in 1144, Eugenius III, was directly and substantially influenced by the man who would become most directly associated with the crusade: Abbot Bernard of Clairvaux (d. 1153), a passionate reformer and Eugenius's former teacher and ongoing mentor. To say that Bernard engineered the crusade is only a slight overstatement. As the leading light in the Latin church at the time, he wrote the major crusading letters, managed the preaching of the crusade, and was its most charismatic and forceful advocate. He expressed the central appeal of crusading with incredible persuasion. For him, this was, as before, a chance for redemption by violently defending and liberating God's land and God's people and defeating God's enemies. It was furthermore an opportunity for those currently alive to live up to the standards set by their ancestors who participated in the First Crusade.

As always, any set of ideas needs a receptive audience. The two most powerful monarchs in Europe in the early 1140s—King Louis VII of the Franks and King Conrad III of Germany—both responded powerfully and actively to the idea of a crusade. However, their courts were markedly less enthusiastic. Bernard's powerful preaching made a difference there, swinging both courts to the idea of crusade.

Historians identify both similarities and differences between the events of 1096–99 and 1147–49. Both crusades shared many ideological themes, the breadth of people who responded to appeals for crusade and participated on crusade, and crusade-related anti-Jewish violence within western Europe. Yet differences can also be identified. First, the crusade of 1147–49 encompassed three different "fronts": the eastern Mediterranean, Iberia, and northern Europe. In the Iberian peninsula, King Alfonso VII of Galicia, León, and Castile followed his mother Urraca's lead and petitioned (successfully) for fighting in Iberia to be considered part of the crusade and entitled to the same spiritual and legal considerations. Meanwhile, German warriors had asked to be able to fight pagans in the Baltic region instead of Muslims in the Mediterranean. Both requests were approved by Bernard of Clairvaux. Second, the presence and involvement of major royal courts marked a change. The First Crusade had been led by loose coalitions of nobles, but all subsequent large-scale crusades to the eastern Mediterranean would be led by monarchs. Third, the crusade of 1147–49 set the precedent of using the military orders to provide leadership and tactical expertise when royal or noble leadership was insufficient.

The fourth and final significant difference concerns outcome. In military terms and from the Latin perspective, the efforts of 1147–49 were a colossal failure by virtually any set of standards one chooses to apply. Although royal, papal, and noble leaders had proactively tried to resolve and prevent the logistical and organizational problems that had plagued the First Crusade, in the end, their actions were insufficient. It surely didn't help that in a moment of dramatic historical irony, no one in Europe bothered to consult with the leaders of the Latin Kingdom of Jerusalem as they made plans. Both the Frankish and German armies opted to take the land route through Constantinople to Anatolia and both arrived in the eastern Mediterranean severely depleted and demoralized. Subsequently a large armed force led by the Franks, the Germans, and the Kingdom of Jerusalem attempted and failed to take the city of Damascus. In the end, the only component of the crusade that could in any way be deemed a success from the Latin Christian perspective was the 1147 conquest of Lisbon in Iberia. All Bernard's dreams ended not with a bang but a whimper. To fully understand why, we need to take a step back and look at developments in the Mediterranean as a whole in the twelfth century.

Further Reading

Bull, Marcus, and Damien Kempf, eds. *Writing the Early Crusades. Text, Transmission and Memory.* Woodbridge: The Boydell Press, 2014.

Chazan, Robert. *God, Humanity, and History. The Hebrew First Crusade Narratives.* Berkeley: University of California Press, 2000.

Cobb, Paul M. *The Race for Paradise: An Islamic History of the Crusades.* Oxford: Oxford University Press, 2014.

Harris, Jonathan. *Byzantium and the Crusades.* 2nd ed. London: Bloomsbury, 2014.

Hodgson, Natasha. *Women, Crusading and the Holy Land in Historical Narrative.* Woodbridge: Boydell & Brewer, 2007.

Nicholson, Helen. *The Knights Hospitaller.* Woodbridge: Boydell & Brewer, 2001.

Nicholson, Helen. *The Knights Templar: A New History.* Stroud: The History Press, 2001.

Phillips, Jonathan. *The Second Crusade: Extending the Frontiers of Christendom.* New Haven, CT: Yale University Press, 2010.

Riley-Smith, Jonathan. *The First Crusade and the Idea of Crusading.* With a new introduction. Philadelphia: University of Pennsylvania Press, 2009.

Riley-Smith, Jonathan. *The First Crusaders, 1095–1131.* Cambridge: Cambridge University Press, 1998.

Webb, Diana. *Medieval European Pilgrimage, c. 700– c. 1500.* Basingstoke: Palgrave, 2002.

III

Shifting Ground: Crusading and the Twelfth-Century Mediterranean

As just outlined, the seeds of crusading ideas fell on fertile soil in Latin Christendom, generating ongoing, if at times qualified, enthusiasm. Nonetheless, the outcome of the crusade of 1147–49 strongly suggests that the geopolitical context for crusades to the eastern Mediterranean had changed between 1096 and 1147.

This chapter explores trends in the broader Mediterranean basin that affected and were affected by crusading in greater depth. The crusader states were only some of many new—or newly reshaped—political configurations that would emerge from one end of the

Mediterranean to the other in the twelfth century. These developments, as well as the continuing evolution and pursuit of crusading activities in Latin Christendom, would come to a head—and to an ironically lackluster denouement—in the eastern Mediterranean crusade of 1189–92.

***

In the crusader states, life both did and did not change for those who now found themselves under Latin rule in the early twelfth century. The immediate aftermath of the conquest of Jerusalem was grim for Muslims and Jews as the Latins tried to drive them out of their newly formed polities. However, it was nothing new to have Christians, Jews, and Muslims living together in the region, and the newly arrived Latins eventually realized that harshly intolerant policies were unsustainable and unprofitable. Following this realization, new Latin leaders adopted some elements of preceding Islamic rule. For example, Muslims, Jews, and non-Latin Christians were assigned a status similar to that of *dhimmis* under Islamic rule. All three groups were legally and socially inferior to Latin Christians but roughly tolerated. In addition, some forms of tax administration and other governmental structures remained essentially the same under Latin leadership.

In other ways, Latins in the crusader states broke decisively with the recent past and signaled their own interests and priorities. To build on the example just given, while Muslims and Jews were required to pay a special poll tax, non-Latin Christians (called "Syrians" by the

Latins) were not. Furthermore, discrete law courts were established for "Syrians" and for minor cases involving different religious and ethnic communities. Extensive resources were dedicated to refurbishing Christian holy places, above all the Church of the Holy Sepulcher, and a new Latin church organization was instituted in the Kingdom of Jerusalem, at the top of the religious hierarchy. While some Latin Christians did emigrate to and settle in the crusader states, in general the Latins were a minority elite ruling over a mostly non-rebellious majority of other faiths.

As the twelfth century unspooled, the crusader states' neighbor to the northwest, the Byzantine Empire, engaged in a delicate dance with all regional actors. Alexios I Komnenos and his successors, John II (brother of Anna Komnene) and Manuel I, pursued the empire's interests by building alliances when possible and winning outright conflicts when necessary. For both Alexios and John II, the primary interest of the empire was not possession of territory or wealth, but rather the traditional goal of Byzantine foreign policy: recognition of the status of the empire and the emperor.[12] The crusader states—in particular Antioch and the Kingdom of Jerusalem—threatened said status, since Byzantine emperors had always claimed the role of protecting Christian holy places as well as the headship of the Christian church in the eastern Mediterranean. Antioch, meanwhile, was not only significant for military and economic reasons, but also as a key bishopric.

12 Harris, *Byzantium and the Crusades*, 79.

From a Byzantine perspective, both Alexios and John II successfully managed the challenge of the crusader states. This challenge was certainly active in the early twelfth century. Bohemond, emboldened by his successes in the late 1090s, attempted to strike in force against the Byzantine Empire in 1107. This unsuccessful campaign resulted in the Treaty of Devol, which dictated among other things that Bohemond was to hold Antioch as the emperor's subordinate. Several decades later, John II led two armed expeditions into Anatolia and the eastern Mediterranean. Both times, he primarily sought recognition of his sovereignty. In 1138, after he overwhelmed the Latin prince of Antioch with superior imperial forces, John II led a coalition of Christian forces against Aleppo, held by the increasingly prominent Sunni leader, Zangi (more on him below). John and his allies did not take Aleppo, but the expedition nonetheless underlined the role of the Byzantine emperor in leading Christian armies in the eastern Mediterranean. A few years later, in 1142–43, John began a formidable expedition that seemed poised to swivel south; John was purportedly interested in a pilgrimage to Jerusalem. What the ultimate outcome of events would have been is unclear, since John died suddenly from an infected hunting injury in 1143. His son, Manuel, then secured the imperial throne.

In the meantime, the pursuit of military *jihad* against Latin and Byzantine forces had emerged in both the rhetoric and internal politics of the Islamicate Levant. The process was slow and uneven, and complicated by the fact that all actors in the region—Byzantines, Latins, Saljuqs, Great Saljuqs, and Fatimids, not to mention

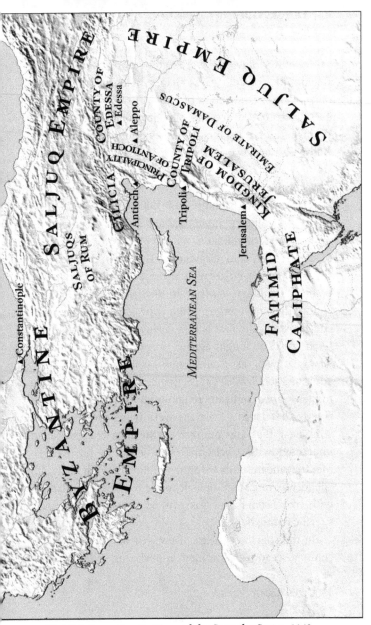

Map 3.1. Byzantine Empire and the Crusader States, 1143.

other minor powers—were often more persuaded by Realpolitik considerations than religious zealotry. And despite the initial shock of the Latin conquests, in the early twelfth century the benefits of alliance with the Latins often outweighed the risks of military *jihad*. This was in part because military *jihad* was an equally valuable strategy when facing Muslim opponents as when facing Christians.

The most passionate and detailed arguments for organized military *jihad* against Latins emerged out of the ranks of religious scholars, in both the eastern Mediterranean and elsewhere. This is not surprising, since religious scholars were the ones actively advocating organized military *jihad* before 1096. But there are several factors that make interpreting appeals for military *jihad* complicated. The first is that, as just alluded to, military *jihad* could be fought against purported heretics within Islam as well as against non-Muslim opponents. In addition, scholars debate whether textual references to military *jihad* indicate religious motivation or, rather, simply that Latin Christians were being fought. Lastly, it is clear that any number of Muslims coexisted and interacted with Christians (and Jews) in the eastern Mediterranean, both before and after the First Crusade; "jihad was not some default mode for Muslim relations with infidels but rather was invoked for specific reasons in specific contexts."[13]

In the specific context of the first half of the twelfth century, gradually swelling appeals for military *jihad*

---

13 Cobb, *Race for Paradise*, 33.

against the Latins enjoyed popular support. Yet when we look at the political leaders who seem to have answered these appeals—and who certainly benefitted from reputations as powerful and dedicated *mujahidun* ("warriors in jihad")—we see men who mastered the rhetoric and energy of military *jihad* in order to consolidate their own political positions. This does not necessarily mean they were irreligious. But it does mean that the history is not one of single-minded, scorched earth opposition to Christians or Latins, but rather, of strategic deployment and reinforcement of the rhetoric of military *jihad* balanced by pragmatic and astute political reasoning and supported, always, by diplomacy and effective military maneuvers.

It may be helpful here to recall the risks of generalization about motives. Few individuals are motivated by one thing alone and few group activities are populated by individuals who are all motivated by the same factors. Bohemond pretty clearly possessed a variety of different motivations for participating in the First Crusade, and that in no way guarantees that his fellow crusade leaders—let alone the majority of crusade participants—shared all or any of these motives. We are in a similar position when trying to evaluate the motivations of twelfth-century rulers like Zangi and Nur al-Din. It seems fair to conclude they too possessed a variety of motivations, and that we cannot say with complete certainty whether others around them or under their command shared precisely the same priorities.

To bring these points to life, let's quickly survey the careers of two major Islamic rulers in twelfth-century west Asia: Zangi and his son Nur al-Din. Both men were members of a Sunni family that rose to prominence through merit and political acumen. Both acquired reputations in their own time and after for their dedication to Sunni Islam and to *jihad*. Both engaged in ambitious maneuvers within a complex and changing political landscape at the eastern end of the Mediterranean.

You'll remember from the previous chapters that the Islamicate eastern Mediterranean on the eve of the First Crusade had been disrupted, in part due to the recent arrival of Turkish peoples who had already converted to Sunni Islam and in part due to a number of prominent deaths in Baghdad and Cairo. The resulting disorientation within the Islamicate world was severe, and this disorientation is usually the first if not the only factor historians use to explain the Latins' success during the First Crusade. Despite the existence of generalized pro-*jihad* discourse before 1100, Islamicate military actions against the Latins in the eastern Mediterranean in the early twelfth century were fragmented and, with the exception of the Battle of the Field of Blood in 1119, largely unsuccessful.

The first major and ongoing Islamicate challenge to the presence of the Latin crusader states was posed by Zangi, the son of a former governor of Aleppo. In 1127 the Great Saljuq sultan named Zangi the governor of Mosul and, in 1128, authorized Zangi to respond militarily to appeals for help from Aleppo. From that point on, Zangi divided his time between consolidating and defending his power base in Mosul and acquiring new conquests in the region. Zangi was singularly successful in his efforts.

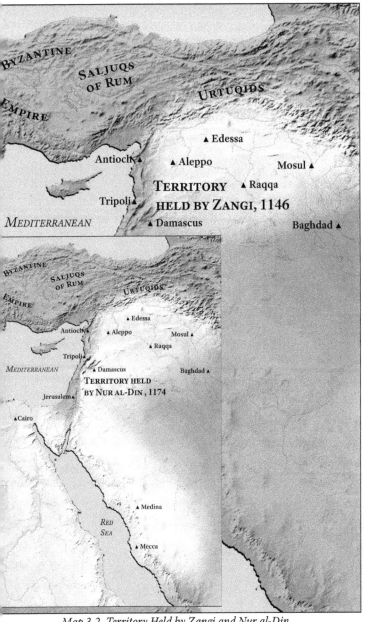

Map 3.2. Territory Held by Zangi and Nur al-Din.

However, it would be a serious mistake to imagine that Zangi was primarily or solely motivated by anti-Christian sentiment. The history of his conquests shows us a man interested in the consolidation and expansion of power at the expense of any and all competitors. At the time, Zangi's main competitors in west Asia were Muslim. Indeed, sometimes he faced Muslim and Christian rivals who had allied together against him. For example, the conquest of Edessa—so easily and wrongly framed both then and now as "a Muslim strike against Christendom"— was a response to a treaty made between the Muslim Artuqids and Joscelin II, Latin Count of Edessa, which surely rang alarm bells in Zangi's mind.

Nonetheless Zangi was known then and now as the first zealous and successful *mujahid* against the Latin presence in the eastern Mediterranean. This is due to the way he was represented at the time and since. Whatever his own personal beliefs or religious priorities, it is certain that those around Zangi commemorated him in terms of the discourse of military *jihad* fought against unbelievers and purported heretics within Islam alike. For their part, Latin and Byzantine accounts did little to downplay the idea.

The career of Nur al-Din, Zangi's second son who was also based in Aleppo, in many ways mirrored that of his father. Like Zangi, Nur al-Din strove against both Muslim and Christian rivals to further increase his power and holdings. For example, Nur al-Din alternately viewed Damascus as a convenient ally or a ripe fruit to be plucked and vigorously squeezed. Like Zangi, he resolutely succeeded in his efforts. Last but not least, like Zangi, Nur al-Din was pervasively commemorated for his efforts as a *mujahid.*

What sets Nur al-Din apart from his father is that we can detect him deliberately and repeatedly employing the rhetoric and practice of military *jihad* and Sunni piety to advance his goals. This meant, among other things, funding major building projects and endowing religious institutions. It also meant cracking down on Shi'ites. It most certainly meant ensuring good relations with the sort of prominent Sunni scholars who could write up Nur al-Din's efforts most effectively. In short, for Nur al-Din, as historian Paul Cobb has so eloquently put it, "jihad was but one plank in a much larger platform."[14]

Meanwhile, the political situation was similarly dynamic in the western Mediterranean. You'll remember that the Almoravids, a pietistic dynasty from north Africa, had entered the Iberian peninsula in the late eleventh century. They picked up land in Iberia from *ta'ifa* kings and continued to maintain control over most of northwest Africa into the early twelfth century. They did not, however, really shift the line between "Christian-ruled" and "Muslim-ruled" Iberia, and Jews, Christians, and Muslims continued to live on both sides of that line.

Early in the twelfth century, the Almoravids' attention turned to an internal problem: the rise of the Almohads, another ambitious and religiously zealous dynasty in north Africa that in its turn claimed the moral high ground. The subsequent decline of Almoravid power led to the reestablishment of small *ta'ifa* kingdoms in Iberia.

14 Cobb, *Race for Paradise*, 45.

The trend didn't last long, however; these new *ta'ifa* kings soon decided that just as the Almoravids had been called upon to help in the late eleventh century, so now the Almohads should be asked to come and lend a hand against Latin Christian-led forces. The Almohads agreed.

Thus in the early 1140s a number of different players contested the Iberian peninsula. The Almoravids (rather, their remnants) were trying to hold onto power. New *ta'ifa* kings were attempting to establish themselves while the Almoravids' control crumbled. The Almohads were supporting these new *ta'ifa* kings with one hand and trying to place themselves in power with the other. Latin Christian monarchs from the north were attempting to expand their own holdings, sometimes in alliance with one another and sometimes not. These monarchs increasingly used the rhetoric of crusade to secure papal support and recruit additional aid for their wars.

Yet crusading rhetoric and religious zeal were not the only factors encouraging Latin involvement in the Iberian peninsula. Political ambition also played a role. Urraca of León and Castile and her son and successor, Alfonso VII, styled themselves "Empress" and "Emperor" respectively, while (Duke) Afonso Henriques became the first king of Portugal, thanks in part to the 1147 crusade conquest of Lisbon. Economics also mattered and economic factors overlapped with both politics and religion. For example, at roughly the same time as he used both diplomacy and military force to subdue Latin Christian rivals in western Europe, Roger II, Norman King of Sicily, embarked upon conquests in Islamicate north Africa in the mid-twelfth century. Roger may have felt piously motivated

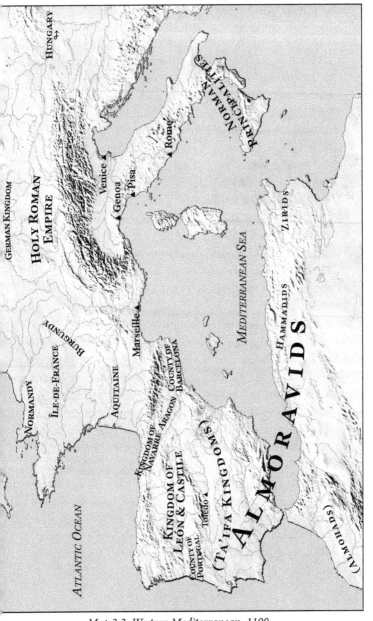

Map 3.3. Western Mediterranean, 1100.

and may equally have been driven by political ambition. It is certain, though, that there were positive economic outcomes from his conquests in north Africa. They struck against pirates based in the region and firmly underlined the importance of Sicily's grain exports to the region, which was at that time in the midst of famine.

To summarize, then, by the early 1140s contemporaries perceived not one but (at least) three Mediterraneans. Muslim observers witnessed Latin Christian conquests in west and east and worried. Latin Christian observers witnessed the successes of Zangi and Nur al-Din in the east, and the Almoravids and Almohads in the west, and worried. Byzantine observers were for the most part content with the way Alexios I and John II Komnenos had managed to reassert the Christian primacy of the Byzantine Empire in the eastern Mediterranean.

The crusade of 1147–49, in particular the expeditions to the eastern Mediterranean, look rather different seen in this light. Instead of a simple story of a wave of united Islamic hostility prompting a renewed and similarly united defense of Christendom—a story we can now recognize as reflecting contemporary polemics on all sides—we see a region continuously contested by actors with a variety of political, economic, and religious goals. Even one type of goal could look different from a different cultural perspective. To give just one example, while both Latins and Byzantines contested various territories, Latins more heavily emphasized actual territorial possession, while Byzantines were more likely to want recognition of sovereignty.

Furthermore, while some Mediterranean alliances were made along religious fault lines, others were not. The singular crusade success of the conquest of Lisbon in 1147 is revealed in part to have been the result of political fragmentation and related opportunities emerging from waning Almoravid power. And the Latins' signal failures in the eastern Mediterranean in 1148–49 are revealed to have been in part the result of the Latins' failure to successfully understand and maneuver within the complex network of alliances and enmities in the region.

None of this is intended to suggest that genuine religious piety was not at play. Clearly, piety was a motivating factor for groups and individuals on all sides of the Mediterranean, and clearly, religious identity mattered. The point is, rather, that religion was not a singular motivating factor, and it was complicated—at least for some, perhaps especially those in power—by political and economic considerations that as often as not encouraged people to think beyond clear-cut lines of religious demarcation.

It is a commonplace to claim that after 1149, crusading morale within Latin Christendom was at a low ebb. While it is true that the period from 1150–85 did not witness any major expeditions launched to the eastern Mediterranean, a number of efforts were made to raise funds or troops for support of the crusader states, while crusading continued apace in northern Europe and, especially, Iberia. There, Almohad conquests in the southern half of the peninsula led to the mid-century establishment of the Almohad Caliphate, with a capital at Cordoba. Due to rivalry among the rulers of northern kingdoms as much as the

Almohads' own military acumen, the Almohads seemed to be ever more permanently settled in Iberia.

In the eastern Mediterranean, meanwhile, by the time of his death in 1174 Nur al-Din had managed to unite and restore Sunni authority in the region, including Egypt. He also empowered the man who would come to symbolize medieval Islamic rule perhaps more than any other: Salah al-Din. Nephew of a trusted Kurdish *amir* who had been dispatched to pin down Fatimid Egypt once and for all, Salah al-Din used his position in the newly-subdued Egypt to vault into power—or perhaps more accurately, to march carefully and decisively into power over his rivals, one strategic step at a time.

Step one was to ensure his base in Egypt. Step two was to position himself as a supporter of Nur al-Din's rightful heir, the child al-Salih Isma'il—and then take control of al-Salih Isma'il's armies in the Levant. Military successes in the region led to step three, a diploma of rights to conquered lands received from the 'Abbasid caliph directly. Step four was marriage to Nur al-Din's widow. When al-Salih Isma'il died in 1181, it must have seemed like just another piece serendipitously falling into place. By 1186, Salah al-Din had subdued his Muslim rivals, recovered from a mysterious yet serious illness, and clearly envisioned the next step. This would be war against the crusader states as a means to bolster his reputation, affirm his right to lead, silence critics who questioned the piety of ongoing warfare against Muslims, and pay his troops. Thus, like his predecessor, Nur al-Din, Salah al-Din used military *jihad* as a plank in a larger platform. This doesn't mean he lacked religious motivation but rather, that we should be careful viewers of the image of a pious *mujahid* created and recreated both for political ends and popular entertainment from the twelfth through the twenty-first centuries, just as we should be careful viewers of constructed images of pious crusaders.

As he focused on crushing Muslim rivals in the second half of the twelfth century, Salah al-Din had naturally made alliances with this or that Latin leader in the crusader states. After he had subdued his Muslim opponents, in 1186 he used a breach in a treaty—a raid on a caravan—as a reason for war with the crusader states. He soundly defeated the armies of the Kingdom of Jerusalem in battle at the Horns of Hattin and from there besieged Jerusalem itself. The city surrendered on good terms in 1187; in deliberate and decided contrast to the reported carnage of 1099, the Latins were given 40 days to ransom themselves and their families, and the Church of the Holy Sepulcher was allowed to stand. In the aftermath, Salah al-Din ensured that his image was firmly cast as the generous *mujahid* who fought against Muslim adversaries only in order to ultimately achieve victory in military *jihad* against Christians, whom he then treated with compassion.

Compassion notwithstanding, news of Salah al-Din's conquest of Jerusalem was met with dismay in Europe. The papacy moved swiftly to call for a major joint expedition to the eastern Mediterranean, but these efforts and genuine popular dismay at the news were complicated by intra-European politics. Admittedly, some Latin monarchs were quick to respond. William II of Sicily sent a fleet to succor Tripoli, Antioch, and

Tyre in 1188, and Frederick I of Germany, Henry II of England, and Philip II of France were all eager to crusade. However, Henry's eldest son, Richard disrupted things in his personal bid for power, alternately supporting and rebelling against his father in conflict with France. (The irony given Richard's later reputation as a crusader is not small.) Henry's death in 1189 and Richard's subsequent coronation as Richard I of England allowed plans for departure of English and French contingents to resume. In the meantime, the Germans had stolen a march, literally, and were confidently moving a massive and well-organized army overland towards Constantinople.

Things did not go well at Constantinople, and to understand why, we need to look at changes in the Byzantine Empire and the crusader states in the later twelfth century. Beginning in 1143, Manuel Komnenos in many ways continued the policies of his predecessors when treating with the crusader states and Latin Christian powers in Europe. In other words, he sought to reassert the primacy of his empire as the preeminent Christian power and protector of the Christian holy places. He brought Antioch under imperial control, negotiated successfully with Nur al-Din, and managed to demonstrate Byzantine overlordship of the Kingdom of Jerusalem while maintaining friendly relations with its rulers. Aware of the anti-Byzantine sentiments swirling in Latin Christendom after the Second Crusade—the empire made a convenient scapegoat for some—Manuel cultivated a Latin-friendly reputation while consolidating Byzantium's position. Not all Byzantines appreciated this attitude towards the Latins, however, and Venetians, who had long taken advantage of unrivalled trading privileges within the empire, were increasingly reviled. Even Manuel himself took actions against the Venetians living in Constantinople in the 1170s.

After Manuel's death in 1180, political infighting in Byzantium led to violence that substantially weakened relations with Latin Christendom. A dramatic coup placed Andronicus I Komnenos on the throne. While Jonathan Harris has successfully debunked the idea that Andronicus and his reign were "anti-Latin,"[15] nonetheless, the new emperor ruthlessly cleaned out the imperial house, and he did not imitate Manuel's careful attention to how his actions appeared to Latins. As a result of this attitude along with coinciding factors, when Andronicus took Constantinople by force in 1182, his troops as well as local residents attacked the Italian merchants in the city, both Genoese and Pisans. Those unable to flee were slaughtered and their neighborhoods were looted and destroyed. Unsurprisingly, this news was received with horror in Latin Christendom. William II of Sicily saw in events an opportunity to expand his own holdings. He launched his fleet against Andronicus and his empire, prompting Andronicus to make peace with the Venetians and ensure he was on a solid footing with Salah al-Din. Nonetheless, Andronicus's reign unraveled in 1185, leaving the young Isaac Angelos—a relative of the Komnenians—to grab the imperial throne as Isaac II.

Isaac II Angelos took charge of an empire that had effectively burned its bridges with Latin Christendom,

---

15 Harris, *Byzantium and the Crusades*, 121–22 and ongoing.

both in Europe and the crusader states, at precisely the moment when Salah al-Din had conquered Jerusalem itself. He also took charge of an empire facing a number of separatist rebellions. As he tried to put out the fires, Isaac continued to pursue diplomatic stability with Salah al-Din. And then he learned that Frederick I of Germany was leading a massive army directly to Constantinople. This was hardly good news, since Frederick was an old enemy of the empire. Isaac tried to use the same strategies as Alexios I had in the 1090s, i.e., managing the incoming Latins while maintaining contact with local Muslim rulers, but circumstances and attitudes had changed. At the end of the day, Isaac did not enjoy Alexios's success with either Latin or Muslim powers. He must have breathed a sigh of relief when Frederick's crusading efforts came to an anti-climactic end in 1190—Frederick died attempting to cross a river in Asia Minor—yet upheaval in the eastern Mediterranean was far from over.

Competition for the crown of the Kingdom of Jerusalem, and complex relationships between powerful Latins in the crusader states and western Europe, directly affected crusading efforts. Some genealogical history is necessary to grasp this point. After Baldwin I's death in 1118, a coup placed Baldwin II on the throne. In 1131, Baldwin II died, leaving royal authority jointly to his eldest daughter, Melisende, her husband, Fulk of Anjou, and their son, predictably named Baldwin. Melisende and Fulk were both strong personalities with the desire and ability to rule; of the two, Melisende would leave the greatest mark on the kingdom, surviving Fulk and continuing to exert dominance even after her son Baldwin III took the throne. (He had to literally take it via armed rebellion against his mother and her allies.) Baldwin III died in 1163, and was succeeded by his brother, Amalric.

Amalric left the Kingdom of Jerusalem in a fractious position when he died in 1174. He had two children with his first wife, Agnes of Courtenay: Sibylla and Baldwin IV. He also had a daughter with his second wife, Maria Komnene (the great-grand niece of John II and Manuel Komnenos): Isabella I. When Amalric died, his son Baldwin IV was a minor, which left lots of room for two factions—Sibylla/Baldwin IV vs. Isabella I—to scheme and maneuver. In 1176 Sibylla married William of Montferrat, had a son (of course named Baldwin), and, after William's death in 1177, married Guy of Lusignan.

Sibylla and her brother Baldwin IV had been relatively closely allied, but he and Guy did not get on well, to the extent that as king, Baldwin overlooked his sister Sibylla's rights to the crown and named her son (Baldwin V) as his heir. Baldwin IV famously died from leprosy in 1185, and Baldwin V—who had always been weak—died in 1186. Sibylla was crowned queen, and after agreeing to annul her marriage so long as she could choose her own husband, she promptly chose Guy and crowned him as her king consort. To summarize, in the late 1080s, the monarchs of the Kingdom of Jerusalem (Sibylla and Guy) faced internal rivals (supporters of Isabella I); the Byzantine emperor Isaac II Angelos was trying to get his house in order and repair the damage done to Latin-Byzantine relations; and Salah al-Din advanced on the crusader states.

Rivals continued to strive for the crown of Jerusalem even after Salah al-Din took Jerusalem itself. Guy, then king, had been taken prisoner by Salah al-Din at Hattin. Finally ransomed, Sibylla and Guy were refused entry into Tyre by Conrad of Montferrat, who had long supported Isabella I. Sibylla and Guy responded by besieging the Muslim-held city of Acre with minimal troops. The strategy worked; so many Latins joined Sibylla and Guy to besiege Acre that Conrad was forced to come to terms. This success came at a cost, however, as Sibylla and their two daughters, Alice and Maria, died of dysentery during the siege. The crusader states were attempting to fight an external threat (Salah al-Din) while also contending with internal conflict over the crown and weakened relations with Byzantium.

When Latins from Europe arrived to crusade in the eastern Mediterranean, they intensified these problems—and added some new ones of their own. Richard I of England and Philip II of France joined Guy in opposing Salah al-Din at Acre, but on their voyage across the Mediterranean their own relationship had been strained. In Sicily, Richard used violence to get his sister's dowry back and more. Richard was then joined by his fiancée, Berengaria of Navarre, and resumed the crusade. This may have infuriated Philip, since Richard had previously been engaged to Philip's sister. When some English crusaders and their goods were held by a Byzantine break-away ruler on Cyprus, Richard seized the pretext to invade and conquer the island. In so doing he also helped generate a justification for assaults on Byzantine lands that would prove influential in coming years, namely, that such assaults were justified if they advanced crusading efforts. As a result of Richard's delays, he arrived at Acre two months after Philip. Richard was considerably richer in both lucre and military reputation but he had weakened his relationship with Philip.

This relationship could only weaken further when, at Acre, Philip and Richard had to take sides on the question of who should wear the crown of the Kingdom of Jerusalem. Since Sibylla and her two daughters had died, the heiress to Jerusalem was Sibylla's younger half-sister, Isabella I. One faction liked the idea of dissolving Isabella's current marriage and remarrying her to Conrad of Montferrat—as would eventually happen—while another faction continued to back Guy, Sibylla's widower. Into this heady political stew sailed Richard (distantly related to Guy) and Philip (Conrad's cousin). The two European monarchs agreed to decide who should really rule the Kingdom of Jerusalem. This assumed, of course, that they could get the city of Jerusalem back.

Despite all this political drama, Richard and Philip and their crusader state allies nonetheless managed to outlast Salah al-Din and his armies and achieve the surrender of Acre in July 1191. In the same month the two European monarchs announced a compromise solution for rule of the Kingdom of Jerusalem that would, like any good compromise, make everyone unhappy: Guy would reign for his life and Isabella I and Conrad of Montferrat would succeed him. No doubt vigorously shaking his head and washing his hands all the way, Philip quietly gave Conrad his half of Acre and returned swiftly to Europe. He left behind any number of Frankish crusaders who doubted

Richard's leadership of the crusade and disliked the agreed-upon compromise. At the same time, Salah al-Din's forces were not entirely thrilled with his leadership, either. Richard had executed approximately 3000 prisoners of war after the surrender of Acre. Among Salah al-Din's forces, a desire for retribution was accompanied by the sense that their leader should have been able to prevent the mass execution.

Richard's advance to Jerusalem was thus hindered not only by effective military resistance from Salah al-Din and the strategic difficulties of the march, but also the fact that Latin forces were not unified under his leadership. Indeed, Conrad of Montferrat and his followers negotiated behind Richard's back with Salah al-Din, even while Richard himself was trying to secure a diplomatic end to the crusade. Illness proved the final straw for Richard, and in 1192, he and Salah al-Din signed a treaty that would last just over three years.

In some ways this was a lose-lose situation. The treaty did not give the Latins Jerusalem, and yet it was not a full victory for Salah al-Din either, who had been shown to be unable to fully defeat the Latin forces; both his resources and his cachet among his own troops had diminished. The only potential winners were Isabella I and her new husband, the crusader Count Henry of Champagne (Conrad of Montferrat had been assassinated). Isabella and Henry confidently asserted rule of the Kingdom of Jerusalem despite the fact that the city itself remained in Salah al-Din's possession.

The events of 1189–92 are remembered and depicted with full chivalric display in histories and modern pop culture alike. Both Richard I and Salah al-Din have been romanticized for centuries now, invested with glamor, charisma, and prowess by generation after generation of writers and artists. The conflict is often colored in epic shades, as nothing less than a civilizational battle between Christianity and Islam. There are deep ironies, therefore, in the actual history. First, any number of intra-Christian fractures undermined the crusade, and intra-Christian jostling strongly influenced its outcome. Second, said outcome was a disappointment for virtually all concerned. Disappointment among Salah al-Din's men was underlined by his death in 1193. Disappointment in Latin Christendom was intensified by the fact that the mid-1190s saw crushing and seemingly decisive Almohad victories in Iberia. Yet Latin crusading enthusiasm did not die following these disappointments, just as it did not die following the feeble outcome of the crusade of 1147–49. Rather, it throve, and soon it would be empowered and expressed in new ways thanks to a vital new pope, Innocent III.

Further Reading

Birk, Joshua. *Norman Kings of Sicily and the Rise of Anti-Islamic Critique: Baptized Sultans.* New York: Palgrave/MacMillan, 2016.

Chibnall, Marjorie. *The Normans.* Oxford: Wiley-Blackwell, 2006.

Christie, Niall. *Muslims and Crusaders: Christianity's Wars in the Middle East, 1095–1382, from the Islamic Sources.* Abingdon and New York: Routledge, 2014.

Cobb, Paul M. *The Race for Paradise: An Islamic History of the Crusades.* Oxford: Oxford University Press, 2014.

Earenfight, Theresa. *Queenship in Medieval Europe.* New York and London: Palgrave Macmillan, 2013.

Eddé, Anne-Marie. *Saladin.* Cambridge MA: Belknap/Harvard University Press, 2014.

Harris, Jonathan. *Byzantium and the Crusades.* 2nd ed. London and New York: Bloomsbury, 2014.

MacEvitt, Christopher. *The Crusades and the Christian World of the East: Rough Tolerance.* Philadelphia: University of Pennsylvania Press, 2009.

O'Callaghan, Joseph F. *Reconquest and Crusade in Medieval Spain.* Philadelphia: University of Pennsylvania Press, 2004.

IV

Allies and Adversaries: Crusading Culture and Intra-Christian Crusades

THE PREVIOUS CHAPTER MADE A FEW POINTS CLEAR. First, the outcomes of crusading in the twelfth century and its future prospects were interpreted in a variety of ways depending on the perspective of the interpreters. Second, while religious ideas and rhetoric played an important role around the Mediterranean, they were not the only motivating factors in play. Third, alliances and conflicts did not fall into the neat grooves predicted by modern assumptions about an ongoing "clash of civilizations." The events of 1187–92 put in sharp relief the ironic difference between the history and mythology of the crusades.

This chapter focuses on Latin Christendom in greater detail in order to expand upon the latter two points. All the crusading events discussed in preceding chapters were supported and influenced by a rich and diverse assortment of ideas and practices that interwove crusading with other aspects of Latin Christian devotion, society, politics, and culture. At the same time, as we have already seen in the case of the relationship between Richard I of England and Philip II of France, crusading was both fueled and complicated by internecine conflict. Different Latin Christian leaders sought control of both crusading and Christendom itself.

***

In 1197, five years after the truce between Richard I and Salah al-Din ended, Henry VI of Germany—son of Frederick I, who had died so anticlimactically in an Anatolian river—launched a crusade to the eastern Mediterranean. He in turn died anticlimactically in Italy before the ships sailed. Just one year later, in 1198, a new pope was elected: Innocent III. Innocent was then in his late thirties, positively overflowing with ideas about, ambitions for, and confidence in his office and church. He was undaunted by apparent setbacks like ominous royal deaths on the brink of crusade. Indeed, he has been rightly deemed the pope who "contributed more to the [crusading] movement than any other individual except Urban II."[16]

When Innocent became pope in 1198, he inherited a well-developed set of crusading theories, legalities,

16 Riley-Smith, *Crusades*, 174.

and practices honed by prior popes, apologists, and canon lawyers over the past century. When Urban II had preached in 1095 and when the earliest writers constructed a context of meaning for the First Crusade in the early twelfth century, many of the details of crusading were still murky. Admittedly, some legal protections and incentives for crusaders had been put in place in the late eleventh century, and the spiritual benefits of an armed expedition-qua-pilgrimage seemed relatively clear to contemporaries, even if they didn't always agree on the exact nature of those benefits. But even after 1099 it was still unclear who could make crusading vows and what such vows entailed, who should have (or could have) control over avowed crusaders, what distinguished an expedition like the First Crusade from other wars (holy or otherwise) or armed pilgrimages, and—of course—how such costly endeavors were to be financed.

In the twelfth century members of the Latin church attempted to pin down a few of these points. "Attempted" is the key word here, since church dictates were not always heeded. For example, the papacy consistently called for individual crusaders to take vows *after* a papal proclamation, but it's clear not everyone agreed. Some continued to think vow-taking was something to be done on a more ad hoc and spontaneous basis. The papacy likewise consistently claimed the privilege to proclaim and supervise crusades. Again, not everyone agreed with this in practice, despite the comprehensive work of canon lawyers who used the whole battery of Christian authorities to prove that war could be authorized only by God or his representative, the pope. Of course, even if there had been theoretical agreement that popes could launch and oversee crusades, the logistics of leading years-long military campaigns in multiple different places did not favor direct papal command. Additionally, even the most idealistic popes might be willing to give post-hoc authorization to a promising campaign that was already underway.

When it came to the theology of the remission of sins, papal and ecclesiastical authority to grant indulgences had increased, while the general theme—crusading was spiritually beneficial because God considered it meritorious—had remained relatively consistent.[17] In the later twelfth century, this theme was joined by the belief that crusading success reflected the spiritual health or lack thereof of Christendom as a whole, not merely those who directly participated.

Innocent III firmly embraced the idea that crusading outcomes reflected the overall spiritual health of Christendom, an entity that he located equally firmly under papal (not Byzantine) direction. All of the crusades he oversaw reflected an overarching concern with the spiritual well-being of Christendom and the role played by the papacy in ensuring it. The varied targets of crusading under Innocent—Muslims, Christian "heretics," Latin Christian political adversaries of the papacy—reflected twin convictions: first, that Latin Christendom faced internal as well as external threats; and second, that the

17 Ane L. Bysted, *The Crusade Indulgence: Spiritual Rewards and the Theology of the Crusades, c. 1095–1216* (Leiden: Brill, 2015), 278–79.

pope should lead the charge against them all. Thus both Innocent's crusades and his substantial religious reforms and initiatives, perhaps most clearly documented in the extensive decrees of the Fourth Lateran Council of 1215, reflected his desire to build a better and more Latin Christendom.

Innocent III established a number of procedures and precedents for crusading that would extend beyond the end of his papacy. He emphasized that while crusade vows were voluntary, crusading was truly a moral requirement for all Christians. He underscored the importance of devotional practices at home, including crusade-focused rituals and liturgies, to help ensure crusading success. He promoted a system of clerical taxation to help fund crusades and starting in the early thirteenth century, he allowed both men and women to fulfill crusade vows through monetary payments. In line with his process-oriented approach, crusade preaching under Innocent became more systematic, detailed, and explicit, as did the legal rights afforded to crusade participants and the financial arrangements that made any expedition possible.

Yet despite the efforts of Innocent III and all the popes of the twelfth and thirteenth centuries, crusading was never truly controlled by the church or the pope, as Innocent would experience the hard way. One reason for this was logistical; crusading depended on lay leaders for financial and military implementation. A second, more profound reason was that the papacy wasn't alone in developing the practices of crusading and considering the ways in which those practices reflected greater truths or deeper priorities. Different members of Latin Christian society—lay and ecclesiastic, men and women—wove crusading into broader and co-evolving cultural patterns.

One such pattern lay in devotional culture. The crusades can be seen as part of a broader phenomenon that historians call "lay piety"—practices and actions taken by the laity in order to express, promote, and celebrate their religious beliefs. Participating in a crusade, either by bearing arms or providing funds and other kinds of support for an expedition, could be one such practice. Other practices—many of which intersected with crusading in one way or another—involved donations of money or land to pious organizations or religious orders, pilgrimage, support for church liturgies or programs of prayers, joining local organizations such as lay fraternities or religious orders, revering relics, and centering religious devotions on the cross and Christ's victory and suffering thereon. Crusading and these other devotional practices intersected with and reinforced each other in a multitude of ways, and this can make it hard to read the particular meaning of a particular symbol, activity, or rhetorical phrase. To give just one example, the cross became the symbol par excellence of crusading, but it was also the symbol par excellence of Christianity more broadly.

Another pattern concerned the moral value of violence. The idea and rhetoric of Christian violence as a moral good was powerful and popular. In the early thirteenth century, Innocent III confidently claimed that crusading was nothing less than "a means of salvation."[18] But crusading was not the only context in which contemporaries sought for a way to perform their customary violence as moral agents. The twelfth century was also pivotal for the development of ideas related to medieval chivalry. The word chivalry comes from the Old French *chevalerie*, a noun which meant a group of warriors on horseback ("knights" in English) and/or a set of behaviors and values associated with said warriors. For our purposes, we can think of chivalry as the idea, developing apace in the eleventh and twelfth centuries, that knightly violence reflected the elite social and moral status of its agents. This violence and its elite moral status were explicitly Christian.

Chivalry and crusading fed and informed each other. This was in part because of shared ideas about the possibility of performing violence as a moral good. It was also because of shared participants and enthusiasts. At the same time, crusading and chivalry were not precisely the same thing and were not performed by precisely the same individuals. Indeed, at times the two cultural patterns were in direct conflict. For example, while tournaments were a key chivalric practice, they were seen by some as a distraction from the "real work" of crusading and other wars.

Economics, too, informed and were affected by crusading. The First Crusade and the establishment of the crusader states had given Italian merchants and their home city-states an important landing stage in the eastern

---

18 Innocent III, *Quia maior* (1213) quoted in Riley-Smith, *Crusades*, 199.

Mediterranean. These landing stages were important not only for their physical location, but also because of the generous political privileges granted to Italian communities by Latin (and at times Byzantine) rulers—privileges they were not granted by, for example, the city of Alexandria.

Arguably both the economic motives of Latin crusaders from merchant communities, as well as their religious fervor, drove participation in crusading—or, at least, affected the ways in which that participation was undertaken. At the same time, as David Abulafia has emphasized, we have to recognize that the crusades did not cause these economic developments, but rather, developments already underway in the eleventh century made crusading technologically possible.[19] And as with chivalry, economics and crusading were sometimes at odds, at least in the eyes of some. From the mid-twelfth century onwards, the papacy attempted to impose boycotts on Mediterranean trade that had the potential to provide resources to the crusaders' enemies. "Attempted" is the key word, since these boycotts were never completely respected nor consistently enforced. At the same time as crusading aligned with some economic trends, crusading aggression was directly at odds with the pluralistic interactions that more regularly defined trade in Afro-Eurasia.

19 David Abulafia, "Trade and Crusade, 1050–1250," in *The Eastern Mediterranean Frontier of Latin Christendom*, ed. Jace Stuckey (Aldershot: Ashgate, 2014), 373–92.

Another cultural pattern connected crusading with ideas and practices of family heritage, especially among social elites. Even during the First Crusade, we can discern patterns of participation that reflected family sentiment and cooperation. Crusade vows were individual, but the effort was—had to be—familial since crusading was a costly endeavor that left one's family and possessions at risk during one's absence. Family support was therefore essential in two ways: first, to help raise funds for those crusading; and second, to ensure the maintenance and protection of family and possessions at home during the crusade. Thus there were quite practical reasons why generational participation in crusading can be traced among families. In addition, however, patterns of family participation in crusading reflects the fact that the family—one's lineage—was a central locus for communication, identity, and prestige.

Indeed, crusading rapidly became a key part of many noble family identities, a proud example of courage, piety, and prowess across the generations. In the first half of the twelfth century, multiple families actively commemorated the deeds of forebears on crusade and linked those deeds with present actions. We can identify conscious callbacks to a family's crusading past in everything from pious donations, the taking of religious vows, the endowment of art and architecture, the writing of family histories, and the pursuit of chivalric reputation in battle, all the way to the ultimate act of imitation: participating in a crusade oneself. Over the decades and centuries to come, participating in—and sometimes dying on—a crusade became a virtually obligatory family tradition for many, performed by each successive generation in turn.

Furthermore, when we examine political dynamics within the crusader states, we see complicated webs of family relationships linking western Europe to the eastern Mediterranean. We've already discussed how both Philip II of France and Richard I of England were related to the two contenders for the Kingdom of Jerusalem in the late twelfth century. Additionally, the family trees of Frederick I of Germany and Melisende I of Jerusalem were intertwined over multiple generations. Likewise, powerful noble families existed and operated alongside and among the royals. For example, it is hard to discuss almost any dispute about government, law, or crusading in the Latin eastern Mediterranean in the thirteenth century without referencing the Ibelin family, which was alternately linked to various thrones by marriage. The crusades were about Christian brotherhood and sisterhood, but they were about actual brothers, sisters, and other kin, too.

Tying together violence, nobility, family, and chivalry were ideas about gender heavily inflected by social class. Latin crusading sources repeatedly emphasized the "manliness" of crusaders and their actions. It's key to recognize that crusading masculinities—like medieval masculinities in general—were plural. Latin Christian men operated in a world with multiple, overlapping ideas of what it meant to be a man. In the context of the crusades, masculinities could certainly be performed through violence, but they could also be performed through self-denial and endurance of suffering, sexual self-control, courage, preservation of family honor, love for one's Christian "siblings," and general piety.

At the same time, crusading was not just a man's world. Women were essential and active agents in virtually every aspect of crusading, though their roles have often been obscured by the biases of the written source record and modern assumptions about medieval women. At the most basic level, women played a significant role in the transmission and encouragement of crusading ideals; family participation has been traced repeatedly to networks of female kin among the noble and royal houses of Europe. Until Innocent III did away with the stipulation, wives had to grant consent to husbands who wished to take crusade vows. Female family members usually needed to consent to—if not directly implement—the sale, transfer, or management of family property and wealth necessary to fund crusading. Sometimes women did much more than consent. Circa 1300, a group of Genoese noblewomen banded together to raise funds and make plans on their own initiative for a crusade; their efforts were endorsed by the papacy.

Women's roles in crusading often included political, military, and family leadership. In the absence of male family members, noble women ruled and protected not only their family but their polities. Additionally, women took crusade vows themselves, and there are examples of queens and noble women leading their own armies on crusade, either alone or side-by-side with their husbands, as Eleanor of Castile and Edward I of England did in the thirteenth century. Meanwhile, in the Kingdom of

Jerusalem, powerful queens like Melisende and Sibylla ruled deftly in their own right.

While the vast majority of our evidence relates to noble and royal women, we do have evidence that women of other social classes were also involved. Written accounts of crusades describe women (in the generic) assisting and supporting armies, even wielding arms in extreme circumstances. We also know that women were abducted, enslaved, tortured, and killed; on no side did crusading violence exclude women and children, as modern ideas about "chivalry" or the treatment of civilians might lead us to expect. Other women (and men) became non-combatant Templars or Hospitallers, joining European houses of these military orders.

In a few cases we can identify the involvement of individual women of non-elite birth in the crusading movement. For example, Saint Catherine of Siena actively advocated for crusading in the fourteenth century; although her religious reputation later granted her considerable social privilege, she was born the daughter of a cloth-dyer. Most notably, an Englishwoman named Margaret of Beverly bore arms and was wounded in the defense of Jerusalem in 1187. Subsequently she was captured and escaped captivity on several occasions. We know of Margaret's story because her younger brother, an English monk named Thomas, wrote an account of her experiences "to the glory of God and for love of his sister."[20] Margaret's story neatly illuminates the interpretative dilemma facing historians who seek to evaluate the history of women and crusading: even when women's experiences reach us, they do so predominantly through men's voices, whether those voices seek to praise, blame, or disregard.

You'll note that all of these patterns are concerned, at some level, with identity—Latin Christian identity, class identity, family identity, gender identity. Perhaps unsurprisingly, then, attitudes towards Jews, Muslims, pagans, and heretics, and ideas about how they should be treated by Christians, also formed an axis of identity that intersected with crusading. While we can outline an overall increase in intolerance and persecution towards all four groups during the period from 1050–1600, there are nonetheless some key differences. In the case of Jews, Latin Christian attitudes moved from general if ambivalent tolerance in the early Middle Ages to active intolerance, persecution, and expulsion in the later Middle Ages. In the case of Muslims, Latin Christian attitudes shifted from rough tolerance, and for a number of Latin Christian intellectuals, respect or envy for the cultural achievements of the Islamicate world, to active intolerance and expulsion. Attitudes towards pagans and heretics remained largely the same: pagans continued to face a combination of Christian missions and violent

20 Thomas of Froidmont, "The Adventures of Margaret of Beverly, A Woman Crusader," trans. Emilie Amt, in *The Crusades: A Reader*, ed. S. J. Allen and Emilie Amt, 2nd ed. (Toronto: University of Toronto Press, 2014), 204–08.

conquest/forced conversion, and heretics continued to be subject to church-sanctioned violence executed by lay authorities. Notwithstanding, later in the Middle Ages these trends were expressed via crusading and buttressed by new ecclesiastical institutions, like the Inquisition. The general movement towards increasing persecution of those deemed deviant has been persuasively linked to the desire to define and secure Latin Christian identity and hegemony. At the same time, it is well worth reiterating that these are broad generalizations on a vast scale. Relations between individuals and faith communities varied considerably, and local factors were often decisive.

For some Latin Christians, all these various elements of crusading identity combined with local or regional sentiments—even what we might call proto-nationalism. For example, from the First Crusade onwards, the Franks self-identified as the crusading *gens* ("people") par excellence. This connection between the Franks and crusading—and in particular, Frankish monarchs and crusading—would be most spectacularly claimed by Louis IX of France in the mid-thirteenth century. On the other side of the Channel, one of the legacies of Richard I's crusading role was to link his reign, and through him the English crown, to crusading. Similar trends played out on a smaller scale in specific counties or localities. They also played out in more all-encompassing ways, beyond monarchy. In twelfth-century Iberia, crusading rhetoric increasingly fused with particularly local concerns and ambitions. In many ways, the second half of the twelfth century witnessed the beginning of war depicted in terms of proto-national as well as religious liberation in Latin Christian Iberia.

All of these cultural patterns met at some points and diverged at others. And all of them were reinforced or propagated by individuals at various levels of society, lay and ecclesiastical alike. It is tempting to imagine a fixed, unequivocal divide between "lay" and "ecclesiastical" ideas, but such a divide doesn't hold up to scrutiny. While there are some precise points on which there was a clear divide between ecclesiastical and lay perspectives—for example, anti-Jewish violence and chivalric tournaments were pretty consistently criticized by members of the church—most of these cultural patterns can be identified in textual and visual/material sources produced by and for both ecclesiastics and the laity. On reflection, this isn't surprising. After all, lay and ecclesiastical elites were often directly related by blood. Ecclesiastical elites were born and raised within lay environments, and the laity were often proactively concerned with their piety, educated by members of the church, and liable to join a religious order later in life. Likewise, those responsible for vernacular literature were primarily educated by members of the church.

It may be especially tempting to imagine that the church promoted more "pious" and orderly ideas of crusading, while the laity were responsible for enthusiastic and gory celebrations of violence. However, the past few decades of research have shown this to be inaccurate in several ways. Members of the church wrote the bloodiest descriptions of the slaughter in Jerusalem in 1099. Members of the church joined the laity in advancing the idea that crusading constituted an act of vengeance. One ecclesiastical account described an abbot calling for indiscriminate slaughter of the people of Beziers in 1209 during the Albigensian Crusade, saying "Kill them all. For the Lord knows who are his."[21] (While this later account may well be inaccurate, it was written from a pro-crusade perspective; in other words, the quote was ascribed to the abbot as a mark in his favor.) Not only was the rhetoric of violence embedded in Christian thought and piety from a very early date—in Latin Christian monasticism[22] as well as both Latin and Byzantine imperial ideologies— but through the Middle Ages, some clerics continued to themselves commit acts of violence, which were judged positively or negatively depending on the motives believed to underlay the acts.[23] The point is not that the Latin church was in some way corrupt or morally deficient, but rather that at this time, ideas of Christian violence existed throughout society, not just among the laity.

It would similarly be a mistake to imagine that everyone was in favor of crusading. There were critics. That said, there wasn't widespread and pervasive criticism, nor was criticism primarily focused on the

---

21 Caesarius of Heisterbach, *Dialogus miraculorum*, quoted in Tyerman, *God's War*, 591.

22 Katherine Allen Smith, *War and the Making of Medieval Monastic Culture* (Woodbridge: The Boydell Press, 2011).

23 Craig M. Nakashian, *Warrior Churchmen of Medieval England, 1000–1250* (Woodbridge: The Boydell Press, 2016).

idea of Christian violence itself. The crusading failures of 1147–49 prompted the most sustained critique, and that critique was directed at how the related expeditions were undertaken. In the later twelfth century onwards, criticism tended to come either from those who were critical of either the papacy or a particular pope, those who had interests in crusading funds being used for other endeavors, or those who felt that crusading was being mismanaged in some other way. In other words, criticism mainly focused on how crusading was implemented rather than on the concept of crusading itself.

Equally it would be a mistake to think that those who supported crusading consistently agreed and cooperated with each other. Crusading was as often a weapon for internecine conflict within Latin Christendom as it was a foundation for unity. The history of crusading between 1100 and 1250 is punctuated by tussles between different Latin Christian leaders who sought to control crusading, Christendom, or some piece thereof. In fact, we've already seen this occur between different lay leaders on crusade or about crusading. On the First Crusade, Bohemond and Raymond IV of Toulouse were famously at odds. Moving into the twelfth century, some accounts blamed infighting between Raymond of Poitiers, Prince of Antioch, and his nephew Louis VII of France for the crusading failure at Damascus in 1148, while Conrad of Germany had taken the overland route due to conflict with Roger II of Sicily. In the later twelfth century, as discussed in the previous chapter, there were significant tensions between Richard I of England and Philip II of France, as well as between contenders for the crown of

Jerusalem. These are just the most notable and obvious examples of an ongoing reality. Such intra-Christian conflicts variously reflected disagreement over inevitable logistical matters and tactical issues, preexisting tensions, concurrent hostilities, or new rivalries emerging in the face of potential risks and rewards.

At the same time, Christian politics in the eastern Mediterranean were similarly complicated, both within the crusader states themselves, between various crusader states and the Byzantine Empire, and between the Byzantine Empire and Latin crusaders from Europe. And of course, the relationship between the papacy and all of the above actors—including lay crusade leaders— also fluctuated. The previous chapters have already given plenty of examples of such complexities, and how they both affected and were affected by crusading. Some may be inclined to conclude that given such clear failures to operate as a unified religio-political unit, Christianity in the period was nothing more than a superficial gloss applied to crass power negotiations. Yet that too would be a mistake. When we look at intra-Christian relations in the medieval Mediterranean, we see that both Realpolitik considerations and central theological issues served as grounds for conflicts or alliances, depending upon circumstances and the individuals involved.

The alternating ally/adversary status of virtually all Christian actors in the crusades demonstrates the complex realities of contemporary warfare, religion, and politics. It furthermore provides a necessary corrective to an imagined Christian unity of the crusades. The many crusades supported by Innocent III and his successors in the late twelfth and early thirteenth centuries serve to underline the point and to further illustrate how crusading was itself a political tool—or weapon, as the case may be—within Latin Christendom.

The crusade of 1202–04 (labelled by nineteenth-century historians the Fourth Crusade) was first aimed at Egypt; it famously wound up sacking the Byzantine capital, Constantinople. The question of why the crusade ended in this way has been debated for a long time in great detail. For our purposes here, suffice it to say that both the initial diversion to Constantinople and the eventual decision to attack the city reflect two main factors: power relations in the Mediterranean and the practical needs of crusading—for transport, for funds, for supplies, and for decisive, on-the-ground leadership. The papacy called for the crusade, but the expedition was in reality led by a number of Frankish and Italian nobles and depended on the economic powerhouse of Venice. Venice and the Byzantine Empire were alternately political and economic allies and rivals, and the exiled-yet-hopeful Byzantine prince Alexios IV Angelos was related to Latin crusade leaders by marriage; he was ready to promise any number of unlikely things in return for help regaining his throne. In the meantime, the crusade was in need of financial resources, and with the conquest of Cyprus in 1191, Richard I of England had arguably set a precedent for justified attacks on Byzantine possessions if doing so supplied a crusade.

The Latin conquest of Constantinople was by no means "fated" or in any way predetermined, but it also isn't surprising given the circumstances and context just noted. It also wasn't universally condemned in the Latin sphere. There were differences of opinion within Latin Christendom and among the crusaders themselves about the conquest, and during events Innocent III was outraged by his lack of control and issued rapid-fire excommunications. Nonetheless, in pretty short order the Latin consensus was that the conquest of Constantinople was a moral good that would benefit Christianity. After all, it "reunited" the churches under Latin leadership, it flooded Europe with a wealth of relics and other Christian objects looted from Constantinople, and it (briefly) established a Latin Empire, which, it was hoped, would aid future crusading efforts in the eastern Mediterranean. Despite all this, some may still be disposed to view the Fourth Crusade as not a "real" crusade. Such a view would ignore the fact that there had been intra-Christian fighting, contention, and conquest framed in terms of righteous violence from the First Crusade onwards, if not before. (Such a view may also imply that a holy war fought against non-Christians is "better" than one fought against Christians.)

Of course, at stake in all such labels as "intra-Christian" is who gets to decide the religious identity of those involved. The Albigensian Crusade (1209–29) was directed at Cathars—heretics from one vantage point, Christians from another—and their noble sympathizers in what we would now call southern France. The papacy had been concerned about the reports of heresy for decades and for almost as long had been trying to entice the northern Frankish kings to crusade in the south. King Philip II was finally persuaded to give his nobles

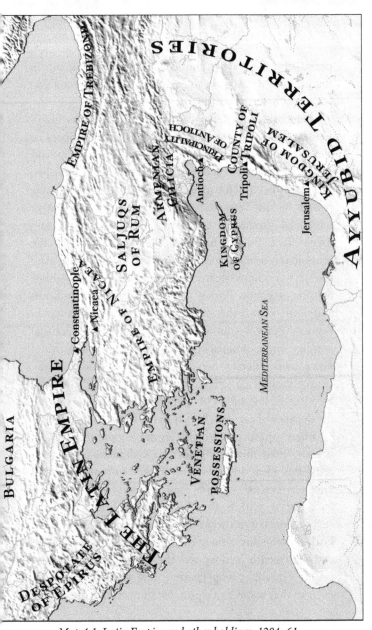

Map 4.1. Latin Empire and other holdings, 1204–61.

permission to act when Innocent III gave participants in the crusade permission to take and keep the lands and goods of "heretics" or their protectors.

Depending on perspective, this crusade was either a pious cleansing of a heresy-infested nest of vipers or a convenient way to expand northern Frankish power and wealth at the expense of a southern region that had previously been all too prosperous. Once it was underway, people in the targeted region viewed it as blatant territorial expansion and most unholy violence, and fought hard and long to defend their homes. Indeed, the crusade was fought especially brutally by both sides, even though or perhaps because in many cases, it was neighbor fighting neighbor. Twenty years of war led to a significant and permanent realignment of power within what would become France: southern regional power and cultural identity were diminished, northern royal and cultural power and influence were heightened. In addition, the church wound up launching the Dominican Order and creating the institution of the Inquisition, because despite the decades of carnage, heresy in the region persisted.

Like the Latin conquest of Constantinople, this crusade is sometimes mistakenly seen as a dramatic change in crusading ideas and practices. It's key to remember that violence against heretics had always been positively encouraged within the Christian tradition. Further, such violence was always supposed to be executed by lay leaders at the direction of the pope. What was new in the early thirteenth century was the specific and deliberate use of crusading to perpetrate this violence, although even in that respect, it's possible to overstate the degree

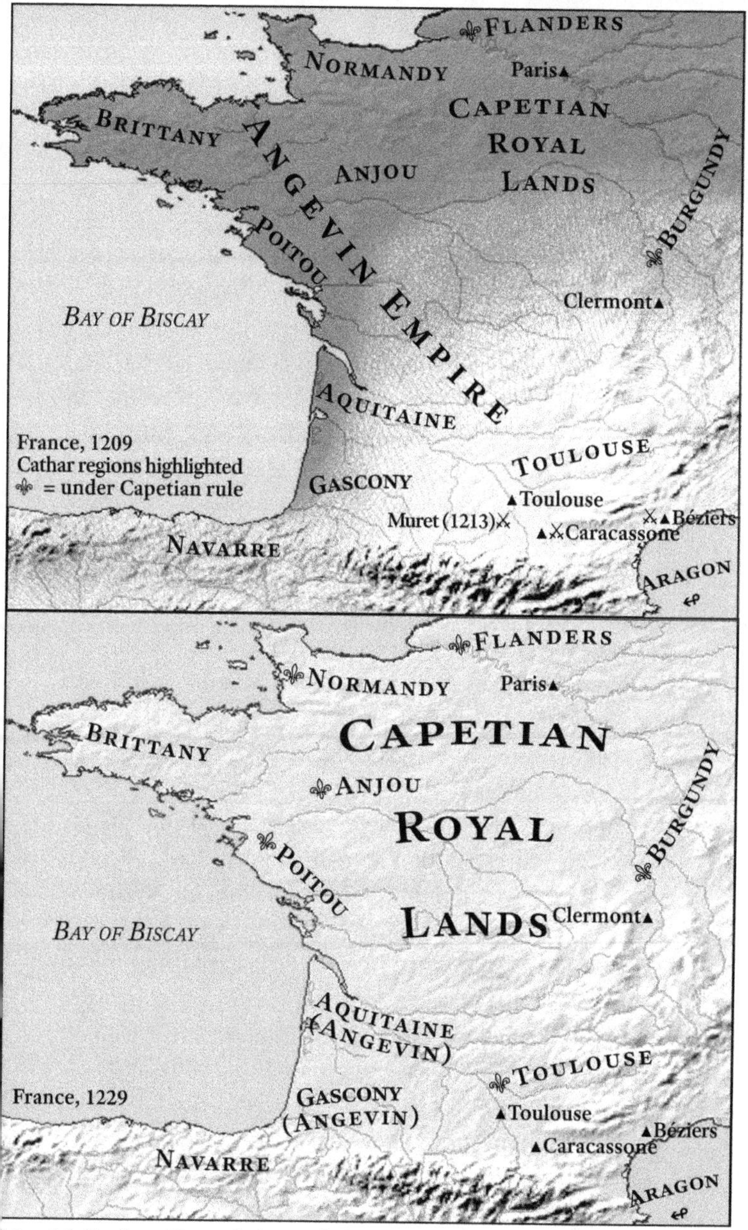

Map 4.2. *Southern France before and after the Albigensian Crusade, 1209 and 1229.*

of change. After all, First Crusade sources tell us about crusaders fighting "heretics" in the eastern Mediterranean in the late eleventh century, and in their letters, crusaders begged Urban II to help them extirpate "heresies" they were encountering. So perhaps it is more accurate to say that what was new was the scale of violence directed at purported heretics—and heretics alone—via crusading.

It's also possible to inaccurately assume that the Latin conquest of Constantinople and crusading in southern France reflect the loss of "true" crusading piety. According to such a view, early crusades (especially the First Crusade) were undertaken by "true" believers motivated by sincere and fervent piety, but as time went on, such pious considerations were weakened by worldly, selfish motivations based on political or economic factors. However, we would have to overlook a lot of historical evidence to approve this interpretation of the past. First, we would have to ignore all the evidence for a range of perspectives and motives for participants in the First Crusade. As already discussed in earlier chapters, even Urban II had pressing and obvious political reasons for launching the expedition as and when he did. Second, we would have to ignore the evidence for a similar range of perspectives and motives in early thirteenth-century crusading. Third, we would have to impose an anachronistic set of values onto the medieval past in order to conclude that religious piety is necessarily distinct from any and all political and economic considerations.

Indeed, the history of the crusades is the history of many connections that may seem surprising to modern eyes. Some of these connections are between analytical spheres that may be considered separate—"religion" and "politics" and "economics"—while others are between regions or peoples thought to have been distant and distinct. The early thirteenth-century crusades remind us that from the start, crusading divided some Christians at the same time as it unified others, and crusades were undertaken because they were considered advantageous— spiritually above all, perhaps, but often politically and economically, too.

All these trends continued to be reflected in crusading to the eastern Mediterranean in the early thirteenth century. The first major expedition after the Latin conquest of Constantinople is usually dated to 1213–21 (and labelled the Fifth Crusade by nineteenth-century historians). Like previous expeditions, it aimed at Egypt. It was unsuccessful from the Latin perspective, and it was not led or substantially powered by the Franks, who were preoccupied by the crusades in southern France. Most ironically, one of the most prominent individuals to take the cross did not in fact participate in the crusade: Frederick II.

The career of Frederick II, King of Sicily and Germany and Holy Roman Emperor, impeccably illustrates the cultural complexities and intra-Christian conflicts of crusading. Frederick II was the grandson of Frederick I and born King of Germany and Sicily in 1194. Deprived of both parents at a very young age, he passed his youth under the ostensible guardianship of Innocent III and the regency or tutorage of various relatives; both lay and ecclesiastical authorities recognized the value of influencing such a fortuitously-positioned monarch. He was crowned Holy Roman Emperor by Pope Honorius III in 1220 after he vowed to go on crusade. His failure to actually embark led many to blame him for the crusade's failure. Singularly unconcerned, in 1225 he married by proxy Isabella II, heir to the crown of Jerusalem and granddaughter of Isabella I of Jerusalem and Conrad of Montferrat. Frederick II embarked on crusade in 1227, only to fall ill and return to Europe; this led Pope Gregory IX to excommunicate him.

Frederick II sailed on crusade again in 1228. Distinctly unamused that he was doing this while excommunicated, Gregory IX excommunicated him again for good measure. Thus twice excommunicated, Frederick negotiated with the Ayyubid sultan, al-Kamil. Although the negotiation's outcome was not a Latin win—see the next chapter for further details—it did achieve a bloodless restitution of Jerusalem to Latin hands in less than a year. Isabella II had died, and Frederick had himself crowned King of Jerusalem before sailing back to Sicily, coolly displacing his own infant son, who was technically the heir.

Frederick's "success" on crusade was praised by a few but viewed as a hostile act by the papacy and their lay allies (Frederick's enemies) at both ends of the Mediterranean. Indeed, Gregory IX and Frederick's father-in-law, John of Brienne, launched crusades against Frederick's lands in Italy while he was still en route back to Sicily. The conflict between the papacy and its allies against Frederick and his allies would ebb and flow over the next several decades, punctuated by excommunications, crusades, and treaties. When Frederick II died in 1250, he had the upper hand in this papal-imperial conflict, though that would not

Map 4.3. Imperial Holdings and Allies, 1250.

remain the case for his heirs. Ultimately the papacy and its allies succeeded in killing off the men of the Hohenstaufen family line in the second half of the thirteenth century.

Thus, we see in Frederick the overlap between lay and ecclesiastical realms. His relationship with the papacy as well as with other lay powers shifted back and forth between alliance and enmity. While he undoubtedly pursued his own interests on crusade, he also valued his piety, or at least his pious reputation; he was reported to have donned the robes of a Cistercian monk shortly before his death.[24] We see also the complicated regional dynamics at play, as Frederick ruled lands in northern Europe, southern Europe, and (briefly) the eastern Mediterranean. The family relationships linking various political actors across generations are clear. Similarly clear is the way in which crusading—whether against Christians or non-Christians—functioned as a political tool for popes and kings alike. Last but certainly not least, in the story of Frederick II we see the many and complex political interactions of the thirteenth-century Mediterranean. It is to these interactions, and their relationship with crusading, that we now turn.

---

24 David Abulafia, *Frederick II: A Medieval Emperor* (Oxford: Oxford University Press, 1992), 407.

Further Reading

Abulafia, David. *Frederick II: A Medieval Emperor.* Oxford: Oxford University Press, 1992.

Brundage, James. *Medieval Canon Law and the Crusader.* Madison: University of Wisconsin Press, 1969.

Bysted, Ane L. *The Crusade Indulgence. Spiritual Rewards and the Theology of the Crusades, c. 1095–1216.* Leiden: Brill, 2015.

Chazan, Robert. *From Anti-Judaism to Anti-Semitism: Ancient and Medieval Christian Constructions of Jewish History.* Cambridge: Cambridge University Press, 2016.

Deane, Jennifer Kolpacoff. *A History of Medieval Heresy and Inquisition.* Lanham: Rowman & Littlefield, 2011.

Geary, Patrick. *The Myth of Nations: The Medieval Origins of Europe.* Princeton: Princeton University Press, 2002.

Hodgson, Natasha, Katherine Lewis, and Matthew Mesley, eds. *Crusading and Masculinities.* London and New York: Routledge, forthcoming.

Kauper, Richard W. *Medieval Chivalry.* Cambridge: Cambridge University Press, 2016.

Moore, John C. *Pope Innocent III (1160/61–1216: To Root up and to Plant.* Notre Dame: University of Notre Dame Press, 2009.

Paul, Nicholas L. *To Follow in Their Footsteps: The Crusades and Family Memory in the High Middle Ages.* Ithaca NY: Cornell University Press, 2012.

Siberry, Elizabeth. *Criticism of Crusading 1095–1274*. Oxford: Oxford University Press, 1985.

Swanson, Robert N. *Religion and Devotion in Europe, c. 1215–c. 1515*. Cambridge: Cambridge University Press, 1995.

Tolan, John V. *Saracens: Islam in the Medieval European Imagination*. New York: Columbia University Press, 2002.

Vauchez, André. *Laity in the Middle Ages: Religious Beliefs and Devotional Practices*. Ed. Daniel E. Bornstein. Trans. Margery J. Schneider. Notre Dame: University of Notre Dame Press, 1996.

Ward, Jennifer. *Women in Medieval Europe 1200–1500*. 2nd ed. London and New York: Routledge, 2016.

V

Changing Circumstances: Crusading in the Thirteenth Century

THE PREVIOUS CHAPTER DISCUSSED THE COMPLEX ways in which crusading was part of broader trends within Latin Christendom in the twelfth century, both implicitly and explicitly linked to politics, devotion, the arts, and social relationships. The reign of Frederick II can serve as an example of these interconnections, and of the way that crusading functioned as a contested field and weapon among Latin Christian powers. But additionally, Frederick's reign encourages us to broaden our view still further and examine crusading in light of the transcultural connections of the thirteenth-century Mediterranean, which was as dynamic and complex as ever.

Admittedly crusading in the thirteenth century continued a number of late twelfth-century trends. Latin Christians continued to pursue crusading enthusiastically on multiple fronts, including well outside the orbit of Jerusalem. At the same time, crusades—especially in the Mediterranean—were affected by the pressures and opportunities raised by new actors in west Asia and especially by intense competition for control of the eastern Mediterranean. By the end of the thirteenth century, the northwestern Mediterranean was increasingly ruled by Latin Christian monarchs, while in the eastern Mediterranean, the crusader states had disappeared.

***

Enthusiasm for crusading among Latin Christians continued to be high and widespread in the thirteenth century. This enthusiasm was particularly apparent at the royal and noble end of the social spectrum. For example, Louis IX of France descended from both maternal and paternal crusading lineages. His piety led him to fiercely pursue royal justice and good rule, the acquisition of holy relics, the condemnation and burning of the Talmud in Paris, and crusading. In his first major crusade—labelled by nineteenth-century historians the Seventh Crusade (1248–54)—Louis targeted Egypt. This expedition, described accurately as "the most carefully prepared and best-organized crusade of all,"[25] failed, and Louis himself was taken prisoner. Days after giving birth, his

25 Riley-Smith, *Crusades*, 221.

wife, Queen Margaret, led the defense of the port city of Damietta before negotiating his release and an end to hostilities with Shajar al-Durr, the female ruler of the Mamluks at the time.

But thirteenth-century crusading wasn't just about monarchs and nobles. We also see crusading enthusiasm at the other end of the social spectrum. At times this was linked to class identities and tensions. For example, Louis's imprisonment sparked a movement of the poor and middling, the so-called Crusade of the Shepherds. Participants in this movement sought to place the blame for the crusade's failure and Louis's capture on noble shoulders.

As in the twelfth century, military leadership on crusade was usually provided by both charismatic monarchs and nobles or military orders—or both. At the same time, the papacy continued to view itself as the supreme leader of any crusade, despite various evidence to the contrary. Louis's expedition to Egypt, for example, occurred while the papacy was itself preoccupied with crusades against Frederick II and his kin; it was not the weaker for it.

Above all, crusading continued to be a versatile tool, easily wielded on multiple fronts and against a variety of targets. The thirteenth century saw crusades against political adversaries of the popes, crusades against Christian "heretics," crusades against pagans in northern Europe, crusades in Iberia, and crusades in the eastern Mediterranean. At the same time, crusading continued to coexist alongside commerce, coexistence, and other modes of warfare. These types of engagement, too, were versatile tools, and as all concerned sought their own advantages—whether political, spiritual, or material—tools were swapped in and out depending upon circumstances and personal priorities.

Most notably, the thirteenth century saw increasingly successful crusading in Iberia and northern Europe and Latin failure after failure in an ever more hotly contested eastern Mediterranean. In some ways this too reflects continuity from the twelfth century; for example, the successes of the crusades of 1146–49 were in Iberia. But at the same time, these thirteenth-century trends also represent changing circumstances in all three regions: northern Europe, Iberia, and the eastern Mediterranean.

As we saw, the first of the many "Baltic crusades" had occurred in the mid-twelfth century and subsequently crusading developed a unique character in northern Europe. In the later twelfth and thirteenth centuries, three related expansionist desires stimulated crusading in northern Europe. First, missionary bishops in northern Europe were frustrated by their failure to make as much headway as they desired. Second, ambitious merchants in northern towns and cities were well aware of the strategic ports and natural resources on tap in pagan-held lands. Third, the monarchs of Denmark and Sweden sought to expand their realms.

The ostensible justification for fighting in the Baltics was to defend fledgling churches and newly converted Christians in the region. Baltic lands were deemed sacred, pagans were decried as enemies of Christ, and familiar crusading themes of defense and liberation were readily adopted. Thus while Jerusalem was seen as Christ's land,

Map 5.1. Latin Expansion in the Baltic Region, 1200–1300.

the Baltic region was recast as belonging to his mother, Mary. By the early thirteenth century, the papacy was willing to grant the same indulgences to crusaders in northern Europe as to those who fought elsewhere. By the mid-thirteenth century, the papacy decided that by virtue of fighting in Prussia one was a crusader and would receive a crusader's indulgence. Furthermore, the papacy empowered others (like the Teutonic Knights) to issue crusading indulgences in certain circumstances. By the end of the thirteenth century, fighting on crusade in northern Europe was represented as service to Mary, represented as a goddess of war.

Thirteenth-century crusading in northern Europe resulted in expansion, settlement, and colonization, as it had elsewhere. Latin colonists settled in the conquered areas, merchants were quick to establish trading outposts, and bishops and monks were equally quick to colonize and build for Christ. Military orders were given quasi-independent status in certain regions, such as the Sword-Brothers in Livonia and the Teutonic Order in Prussia. Other conquered regions were simply claimed by the monarchs of Denmark or Sweden as their own. Although intra-Christian conflicts featured in northern Europe crusading as elsewhere, these conflicts didn't prove fatal; Latin Christian expansion in northern Europe rolled on as the thirteenth century came to a close.

The western Mediterranean was also in flux in the first half of the thirteenth century. By the 1190s the Almohad Caliphate seemed permanently ensconced in Iberia. Alfonso VIII of Castile tried to advance in 1210, only to be slapped back by the Almohads at Salvatierra. Nonetheless,

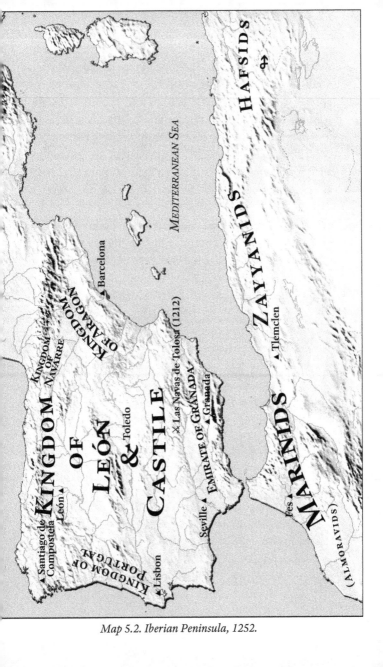

Map 5.2. Iberian Peninsula, 1252.

sensing opportunity, in 1212 Pope Innocent III announced a new crusade in support of Alfonso VIII's efforts. This appeal was met with enthusiasm and crusaders led by Alfonso won a surprise victory at the Battle of Las Navas de Tolosa in July of the same year. In the years following, crusading in Iberia would be alternately sanctioned by an optimistic papacy or discouraged by popes worried about losing resources for crusading in the eastern Mediterranean.

Despite this papal ambivalence, Latin Christian expansion in Iberia continued to gather steam in the thirteenth century. Spurred not only by crusading ideas and papal legitimation but also by political and economic ambitions, and supported by regional Iberian military orders as well as their own knights and mercenaries, the rulers of Aragon and Castile continued to consume Muslim-ruled areas whether or not a crusade had been announced. By 1252, all but the southeastern corner of the peninsula was under the control of one Latin Christian ruler or another. Yet by 1252 that small corner had been firmly buttressed by the Marinids, a new Sunni dynasty that supplanted the Almohads. The line drawn in 1252 between Latin Christian and Islamic rule in the peninsula remained pretty firmly in place through the rest of the century. At the same time, the connection between crusading and proto-national identity in Latin Christian Iberia, and the ambitions of the kingdoms of Aragon and Castile in particular, grew ever more substantial.

Meanwhile, the eastern Mediterranean was undergoing changes of its own. The creation of the crusader states had altered the eastern Mediterranean in the early twelfth century. In the early thirteenth century, the Latin conquest of Constantinople in 1204 reoriented the eastern Mediterranean yet again. In the aftermath of the 1204 conquest, the short-lived Latin Empire (1204–61)— the Latin Occupation, from the Byzantine perspective— was established. Spiritual and material riches flowed in a mighty stream from Constantinople to western Europe, especially to Venice.

Indeed, despite controlling less land area than before, in the early thirteenth century Latin interests in the eastern Mediterranean were doing well. This was in part due to the diversity of lands and settlements either held by Latins or friendly to their interests. Most of these small polities were only loosely allied with each other, if that, but a keen political eye would have seen the potential for political unification. This was even more than usually desirable, since Asiatic overland trade routes had shifted slightly north, increasingly bypassing Egypt in favor of cities farther north. As a mercantile force, Acre had begun to seriously rival, if not surpass, Alexandria.

These economic and political opportunities in the early thirteenth-century eastern Mediterranean helped drive Frederick II's interest in the Kingdom of Jerusalem. More specifically, they inspired his interest in taking control of Jerusalem without the disruption, destruction, and cost of warfare. The fact that Frederick made his move in the eastern Mediterranean while excommunicated ensured the papacy's enmity, since the popes, too, recognized the opportunity at hand. They too could envision a Latin Christian empire in the eastern Mediterranean that would acknowledge papal supremacy and expand far beyond the lands held by the current Latin Empire. Since Frederick II was clearly uninterested in subordinating himself to the papacy—and since he had his own territorial ambitions—he and his allies and heirs became a crusading target, as discussed. While Latin Christians responded to these calls for crusade against Frederick, the church taxation necessary to pay for them was unpopular, and some monarchs—like Louis IX of France—remained committed to crusading in the eastern Mediterranean.

Even so, that did not mean that volunteers eagerly lined up to crusade in defense of the Latin Empire itself. Both the leaders and finances of the Latin Empire were weak. While this encouraged some knights and contingents to step briskly towards Constantinople in the early thirteenth century, enthusiasm for crusading in support of the Latin Empire would not survive renewed threats to Jerusalem. And as the Latin Empire teetered, Byzantine leaders at the rival courts of Nicaea and Epiros began to sketch out their claims to imperial title and rule, asserting themselves firstly against the Latins and secondly against each other.

It was the court of Nicaea that would eventually restore the Byzantine Empire and establish the last Byzantine imperial dynasty, the Palaiologoi. The driving force behind Nicaean success was John III Vatatzes. Between 1221 and 1254 John combined military acumen and battlefield victories with other strengths: wealth based on agricultural surplus and prudent financial policies; a confident reassertion of traditional imperial ideologies; and diplomatic dealings with all available actors. In the end, however, one of his generals—Michael

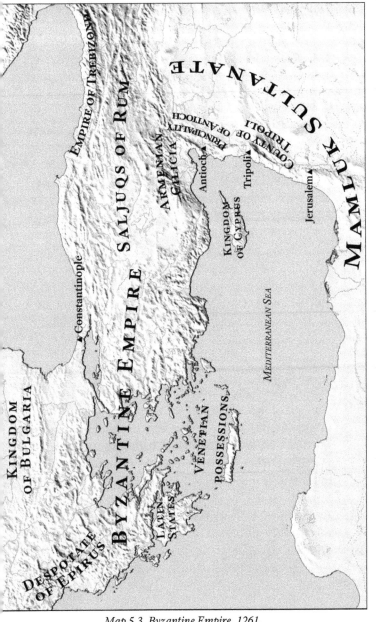

Map 5.3. Byzantine Empire, 1261.

Palaiologos, henceforward Michael VIII—reconquered Constantinople itself in 1261 and quickly established treaties with Genoa in order to thwart their old mutual enemy, Venice.

Notwithstanding this resurgent Byzantium, some European rulers continued to see an attractive opportunity in both the prosperous eastern Mediterranean and the papal assault on Frederick II. Louis IX's younger brother, Charles of Anjou, was both ambitious and capable. He also welcomed collaboration with the papacy. As Charles sought to expand his own power, he accepted a treaty with Pope Urban IV in 1263 that gave him the crown of Sicily in theory. In practice, Charles's military conquest of the island was only complete in 1269. In the 1260s and 1270s Charles claimed overlordship of various Latin holdings in the eastern Mediterranean, and prepared a military assault on resurgent Byzantium, deliberately framing his claims with the rhetoric and ideology of crusading.

Charles of Anjou was thus poised to consolidate and reassert Latin power in the eastern Mediterranean with papal support. He was, however, outmaneuvered by adversaries to west and east. Byzantine emperor Michael VIII deftly distanced Charles from the papacy by making generous and immediate religious concessions that brought together the Latin and Greek churches on terms favorable to Rome. Charles's campaign against Byzantium may have been intended as a crusade, but this new friendship between Rome and Constantinople undercut those intentions decisively.

Charles also failed to reckon with discontent among his subjects on Sicily, which was almost certainly directly encouraged by both Michael VIII and the monarchs of Aragon: Constance, daughter of Frederick II, claimed the Sicilian crown, while her husband, Peter III, was the eldest son of the aggressive James I "the Conqueror" of Aragon. In 1282, discontent in Sicily boiled into rebellion against Angevin-French rule (and papal interference). Once underway, the insurgence quickly escalated. Helped along with Byzantine gold, the Aragonese took the island of Sicily in the same year, and until 1302, wars (often crusades) ground on over possession of Sicily. By then, this mattered little to Charles of Anjou himself. In 1285 he had died, having realized neither his own nor the papacy's dreams of empire in the eastern Mediterranean. In fact, six short years later the last remaining piece of the crusader states, the city of Acre, was no longer under Latin rule.

Why did crusading in the eastern Mediterranean continue to meet with such resounding failure? The problem was not a lack of enthusiasm for crusading, as was once thought. Crusading as a cultural and religious expression remained popular at all levels of society. Logistics, taxation, and planning of crusades had all improved. And while admittedly crusades within Europe—against adversaries of the papacy, against "heretics"—required funds and manpower, it is hard to argue that this fatally underequipped crusading in the eastern Mediterranean. After all, Louis's crusading in the 1240s and 1250s had been spectacularly well planned and equipped, and nonetheless unraveled. To understand the Latin loss of Acre in 1291, we need to look to other factors, most importantly the emergence and success of the Mamluk Dynasty in the later thirteenth century.

After Salah al-Din's death in 1193, the lands he had conquered did not function as a unified whole. Various regions were governed by various members of Salah al-Din's family, the Ayyubids, with the strongest individual at any given time acclaimed as sultan and Egypt recognized as the heart of Ayyubid domains. The Ayyubids' primary concern was not to further eat away at the weakened crusader states, but rather, to successfully defeat rivals within the family and to ensure that no further expeditions from Latin Christendom arrived to disrupt the status quo.[26] The latter was a real threat. The crusade of 1213–21 was very nearly a catastrophe for the Ayyubids, but they rallied and unified to deal with the threat, and—helped by the Nile, whose flooding managed to surprise to the crusaders—they emerged relatively unscathed.

Freed from that external threat, in the 1220s prominent Ayyubids returned to jockeying for power amongst themselves. In doing so they made use of both military might and diplomacy, as had Zangi, Nur ad-Din, and Salah al-Din. Also like their predecessors, the Ayyubids found helpful leverage in alliances with various Christian powers. But whereas in the twelfth century Muslim rulers primarily allied themselves with the Byzantine Empire or a crusader state, in the thirteenth century the strongest potential Christian allies were located further west. And while European rulers did not particularly incline to such alliances in the twelfth century, in the thirteenth century some saw the possible advantages. Furthermore, some Europeans recognized the contests for power within the

26 Cobb, *Race for Paradise*, 204.

Ayyubid world and were willing to directly engage in these contests to advance their own individual causes.

A few examples can help bring these points to life. First, in the 1220s, al-Kamil, the Ayyubid sultan based in Cairo, worried about the threat posed by his brother who was based at Damascus. Al-Kamil turned to Frederick II as a potential ally, offering alliance on generous terms. Frederick II, in need of allies himself, accepted. This diplomacy paved the way for Frederick's non-violent crusade. But by the time Frederick arrived in Jerusalem to affirm the precise terms of the treaty, things had changed. The brother had died and al-Kamil's position was much stronger, while papal opposition had weakened Frederick's position. Al-Kamil thus negotiated an alliance that was a clear win for him and the Ayyubids, though admittedly the popular response to the treaty was overwhelmingly negative.

The reign of al-Kamil's heir followed a similar pattern and confirms the same larger points. By 1234 Pope Gregory IX could see the end of Frederick II and al-Kamil's treaty on the horizon and preemptively issued a call for a crusade; enthusiastic crusaders arrived in the eastern Mediterranean in 1239 and 1240. Meanwhile, in 1238 al-Kamil had died, and had been succeeded as sultan by his son, al-Salih Ayyub. Al-Salih Ayyub's most serious rival was his uncle, the lord of Damascus.

Thus once again Cairo and Damascus faced off against each other, and again European allies proved pivotal. The lord of Damascus was the first to turn to European allies for support, offering back substantial lands in the eastern Mediterranean, including Jerusalem. But al-Salih

Ayyub was not idle. As sultan, he had amassed armies through two traditional means: a corps of mamluk ("slave") soldiers, and nomadic allies. Additionally, he ensured the support of a Turkic people from central Asia who had been pushed westwards—the Khwarazmians. The Khwarazmians proved committed associates. They plowed through Palestine in 1244, taking Jerusalem. The contest between al-Salih Ayyub and his uncle came to a head later that year, when al-Salih Ayyub and the Khwarazmians trounced his uncle and allies. This defeat, combined with accounts of the Khwarismian conquest of Jerusalem, may have helped prompt Louis IX's crusade in the late 1240s. It also meant European attention was firmly focused on Jerusalem, which helped the Byzantines retake Constantinople, as already described.

Louis's crusade, in turn, affected the creation of a new Islamic power in the eastern Mediterranean. Sultan al-Salih Ayyub died in 1249. While his heir returned to Egypt from Mesopotamia, his wife, Shajar al-Durr, effectively governed, colluding with chief ministers and generals to hide the sultan's death. Shajar al-Durr and the aforesaid generals and ministers had mopped up the crusade by the time the formal heir—Turanshah—arrived to accept Louis's surrender and take power. The Egyptian Ayyubids were not impressed when Turanshah's first move was to try to remove them and put his own subordinates into power, and Turanshah was killed in 1250. Shajar al-Durr herself emerged relatively victorious from the whole sequence of events. She ruled in her own name for three months and then married and grudgingly shared (some) power with her husband, the commander Aybak.

Thus began what historians call the Mamluk Dynasty or Mamluk Sultanate (1250–1517).

It's worth pausing here to underline what this sequence of events has demonstrated. At the same time as ambitious popes and European princes were eyeing up the possibility of empire in the eastern Mediterranean, Islamicate polities in the region were in flux. Ambitious Europeans and rivalrous Ayyubids allied and fought with each other. Both diplomatic and military interactions had a wide range of effects around the Mediterranean, not least helping enable the Byzantine Empire's restoration and the rise of the Mamluk Dynasty. The Mediterranean remained complex, dynamic, and subject to change.

Indeed, what ultimately cemented Mamluk rule was the way they handled the newest presence in west Asia: the Mongols. The Mongols were a nomadic, horse-riding people from central Asia. Driven by the ambitions of their leader Chinggis (Genghis) Khan and fueled by a pressing need for grass thanks to a changing climate, they expanded westwards and eastwards. The resulting Mongol Empire (1206–94) was the largest contiguous land empire in human history, with unprecedented impacts on the entire eastern hemisphere. Both the destruction and terror of their expansion and the opportunities and prosperity of their heyday, sometimes referred to as the *Pax Mongolica*, reshaped the eastern hemisphere.

Latin Christians in Europe and the crusader states responded to the Mongols alternately with hope and fear. Perhaps the Mongols were Christians, or perhaps they were pagans who could be converted. If so—or perhaps, even if not—they might be allies against Islamic powers.

At the same time, when the Mongols posed a clear threat to Latin Christendom, crusades were launched against them.

For their part, the "Islamic powers" in the 1250s were dangerously divided until the Mongol threat afforded an opportunity for the Mamluk Dynasty to cement its rule. The Mamluks who had first taken power in 1250 found themselves shoved to west Asia where they rubbed shoulders with a few remaining Ayyubids. The Mongol advance, however, helped elevate three leaders: the Ayyubid prince of Damascus, his chief commander, Baybars, and the Mamluk *amir* Qutuz in Cairo. The Mongols took Baghdad in 1258, formally ending the by-then figurehead 'Abbasid caliphate. Both Damascus and its prince fell in 1260. Recognizing the peril, Baybars and Qutuz led a combined force in military *jihad* against the Mongols and the Mongols' various Christian and Muslim allies—and won. Once Baybars and others subsequently killed Qutuz, a rough consensus elevated Baybars to the role of sultan at the head of a powerful and now unified Mamluk force. The Mamluk Sultanate had survived.

For the crusader states, this meant they had, at best, moved from the frying pan to the fire. As described earlier in this chapter, they had been in a relatively strong economic position at the start of the thirteenth century, but constitutional crises had led to factional infighting and civil war in the Kingdom of Jerusalem. These conflicts were the backdrop to Frederick II's claim to the crown of Jerusalem in the 1220s and Charles of Anjou's outright purchase of the crown in 1277; of course, both times, the city and throne of Jerusalem were not actually under Latin

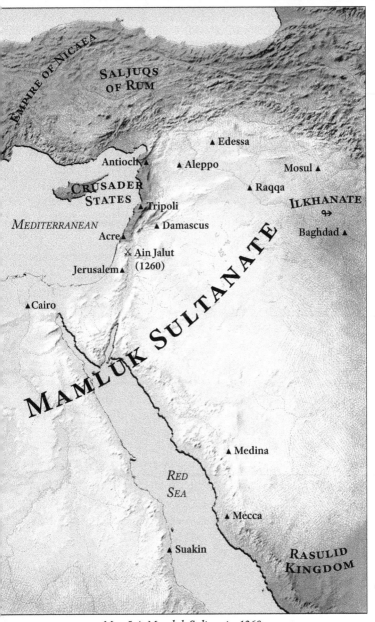

Map 5.4. Mamluk Sultanate, 1260.

Christian control. But it was not only political position and power that were contested. The Italian city-states had also ramped up their rivalries, each seeking primary claim to trade wealth from port cities like Acre and Tripoli. All the while, this wealth began to diminish in the later thirteenth century, as trade routes shifted yet again in the aftermath of the Mongol conquests, further north towards the Black Sea. When the Mongols showed up on the shores of the eastern Mediterranean, the situation fractured further, as some Christians and Muslims in the region eyed up the odds and allied with the Mongols.

Unfortunately for the crusader states, once Baybars had secured his base of power in Cairo and Egypt, he decided that the best way to consolidate and enrich his position was to control the eastern Mediterranean. For Baybars, as it had for Zangi, Nur ad-Din, and Salah al-Din, this meant dealing with both Muslim and Christian adversaries once and for all. The fact of the matter was, however, that Baybars had already mostly crushed Muslim opposition, and so he focused predominantly on conquering the crusader states. This would have the additional benefit of underscoring his legitimacy as a *mujahid* and pious ruler.

Baybars was successful through a combination of diplomacy and military force. Diplomacy helped ensure Latin polities in the eastern Mediterranean remained isolated. He formed alliances with Charles of Anjou, the newly reinstated Byzantine emperors, and the city-state of Genoa in the 1260s. At the same time as he campaigned against one crusader state he skillfully negotiated with another. Thus he divided and conquered. By the time of his death, only Tripoli and Acre remained—nominally—under

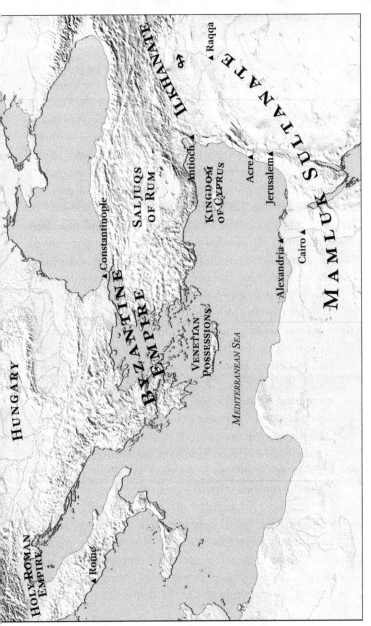

Map 5.5. Eastern Mediterranean, 1300.

Latin rule. Baybars's successors used similar tactics to take Tripoli in 1289 (ironically at the request of the Venetians in the city) and Acre in 1291, six years after the death of Charles of Anjou. This was the nail in the coffin of any imagined Latin Empire in the Mediterranean.

The reason for continuing crusading failures in the eastern Mediterranean thus rests in a combination of factors: shifting trade routes; economic and political rivalries within Latin Christendom; and the presence of new powers like the Mongols, Mamluks, and resurgent Byzantines. We also have to recognize the importance of the eastern Mediterranean in the eastern hemisphere as a whole. It was and had been such contested territory not only because of its religious importance but also because of its role in Afro-Eurasian trade and west Asian politics.

It may seem accurate to paint the 1291 loss of Acre in melodramatic and tragic tones. In such a picture, by the late thirteenth century crusading had become nothing more than another form of international relations, composed of warfare and diplomacy as seemed best at any given time, without the "pure" religious zeal and unified endeavor of earlier, "real" crusades. In this picture, "corruption" of the crusade ideal left Latin Christendom divided and ineffective, doomed to failure, unable to claim the spiritual prize of Jerusalem.

However, in addition to problematically praising and glorifying "pure" holy war, such a picture vastly and inaccurately simplifies crusading history. When we look at crusading in the late thirteenth century, we do not see a drop in crusade enthusiasm or piety among participants. Indeed, we continue to see the deliberate construction of crusading as a devotional undertaking and route to salvation. Furthermore, if we look honestly at the First Crusade and crusading in the twelfth century, we don't see many more signs of actual Christian unity or "pure" intentions in the events themselves. The crusader states formed in the plural because of disunity and rivalry among their founders; Urban II appealed to nobles rather than monarchs in part because of ongoing papal-imperial conflict; Alexios I Komnenos and the Normans fought each other directly before and directly after the First Crusade.

Furthermore, contrary to any imagined tragic narrative, crusading did not end in 1291. Not even Latin Christian political presence in the eastern Mediterranean ended in 1291, since the Kingdom of Cyprus remained strong. Indeed, as the next chapter shows, crusading itself would continue to be enthusiastically pursued and promoted within Latin Christendom and at its frontiers even when faced with environmental change, the Hundred Years' War, and a hemispheric pandemic.

Further Reading

Amitai-Preiss, Reuven. *Mongols and Mamluks: The Mamluk-Ilkhanid War, 1260–1281*. Cambridge: Cambridge University Press, 2005.

Backman, Clifford R. *The Decline and Fall of Medieval Sicily: Politics, Religion, and Economy in the Reign of Frederick III, 1296–1337*. Cambridge: Cambridge University Press, 2002.

Christiansen, Eric. *The Northern Crusades*. 2nd ed. New York: Penguin, 1998.

Gaposchkin, M. Cecilia. *The Making of Saint Louis: Kingship, Sanctity, and Crusade in the Later Middle Ages*. Ithaca, NY: Cornell University Press, 2010.

Epstein, Steven A. *An Economic and Social History of Later Medieval Europe, 1000–1500*. Cambridge: Cambridge University Press, 2009.

Fancy, Hussein. *The Mercenary Mediterranean: Sovereignty, Religion, and Violence in the Medieval Crown of Aragon*. Chicago: University of Chicago Press, 2016.

Housley, Norman. *The Later Crusades, 1274–1580: From Lyons to Alcazar*. Oxford: Oxford University Press, 1992.

Jackson, Peter. *The Mongols and the Islamic World: From Conquest to Conversion*. New Haven, CT: Yale University Press, 2017.

Morgan, David. *The Mongols*. 2nd ed. Oxford: Wiley-Blackwell, 2007.

VI

Towards Christian Nationalism: Crusading into the Early Modern Period

AS THE LAST CHAPTER SHOWCASED, THROUGHOUT THE thirteenth century, the Mediterranean was a dynamic and contested space, and crusading continued to be one of the ways in which Latin Christians engaged in it. In terms of where crusades were waged, where they were successful, and the enthusiasm with which they were pursued, crusading continued along well-worn paths. Even so, two factors distinguished thirteenth-century crusading. First, it was ever more closely aligned with nascent national identities, and second, it was more deliberately connected to political disputes in the Islamicate world. Circa 1300, a Latin Christian presence remained in the eastern Mediterranean and would grow; crusading was rolling on in northern Europe; and enthusiasm for crusading was high.

In fact, as this chapter shows, as both a cultural phenomenon and as a mode of warfare, crusading continued to thrive and exert influence in the later Middle Ages and early modern period—notwithstanding the pressures of environmental change, a hemispheric pandemic, the Hundred Years' War, and religious upheavals within Latin Christendom. Crusading also continued to evolve to suit the times. It found stimulus in not only the successes of the Mamluks and the Mongols, the rise of the Ottoman Empire, and the emergence of an aggressive Lithuanian nation, but also intra-Christian conflicts, the rise of new Christian "heresies," and the expansion of European empires in the Americas. In some regions, crusading ideas and practices played key roles in early modern nation-building.

***

The period from roughly 1300 to 1600 witnessed profound changes in European, Mediterranean, and world history. Within Europe, the series of conflicts known as the Hundred Years' War (1337–1453) shifted the way war was waged—towards professionalization and standing armies—and reinforced the emergence of the early modern nations of England and France. Meanwhile, the Avignon Papacy (1309–78) and the Great (Western) Schism (1378–1417) aroused discontent with the way the

Latin church was carrying out its mission, a discontent that at times deteriorated into division. Centuries later, the Protestant Reformations and wars of religion of the sixteenth and seventeenth centuries also expressed religious discontent and division. These developments affected and were affected by the growth of political ideologies and cultural trends that emphasized the value and potential of humanity, and the supremacy of lay monarchs over the church.

All of the above phenomena were also linked to broader disruptions in the eastern hemisphere. The MCA (Medieval Climatic Anomaly) that had so boosted European prosperity starting in the tenth century finally wound down in the later thirteenth century, ushering in centuries of cooler temperatures in western Europe that are sometimes referred to as the Little Ice Age. The cooling may have seemed gradual at first, but it hit Europeans hard in the early fourteenth century. Six years of cold and incredibly rainy weather between 1315 and 1321 led to widespread flooding and famine so severe it is still known in European history as the Great Famine. At almost exactly the same time, between 1314 and 1321, a cattle plague swept Europe, killing livestock already weakened by cold, floods, and insufficient grain. Like grim icing on a terrifying cake, the hemispheric pandemic commonly known as the Black Death swept Afro-Eurasia from 1346 to 1353. It was followed by repeated episodes of plague through the fourteenth century in western Europe and through the early modern period in the eastern Mediterranean.

To say there was a lot going on would be an understatement, and one might think that crusading would fade away in the face of it all, or at least take a back seat. The opposite is true. Crusading continued to be supported by popular culture and social habits at all levels of European society, both with and without "official" encouragement and sanction from popes or monarchs. Even between 1345 and 1347—at the start of the Black Death and a decade into the Hundred Years' War—a crusade led by the Venetians sailed to defend Smyrna. The Black Death itself, which caused population levels in western Europe to drop so low they didn't recover until the sixteenth century, led to a crusading hiatus of a mere decade. In 1359 crusade preaching and fighting resumed in earnest, fired by the passionately committed Peter I of Cyprus and his allies.

Why did crusading continue to thrive? The first part of the answer lies in the purportedly defensive stance of crusading: "crusading thrived on disasters."[27] Perhaps it is more accurate to say that crusading thrived one way or another, since disasters and perceived threats provided a reason to rally while successes provided a reason to continue. In any event, in the later Middle Ages there were a number of perceived threats, both new and newly resurgent. In the eastern Mediterranean, the Mongols, Mamluks, and Ottomans were successive crusading targets, while the assertive and newly organized nation of Lithuania and the solidly entrenched Kingdom of Granada provided foci for crusading in northern Europe and Iberia

27 Riley-Smith, *Crusades*, 295.

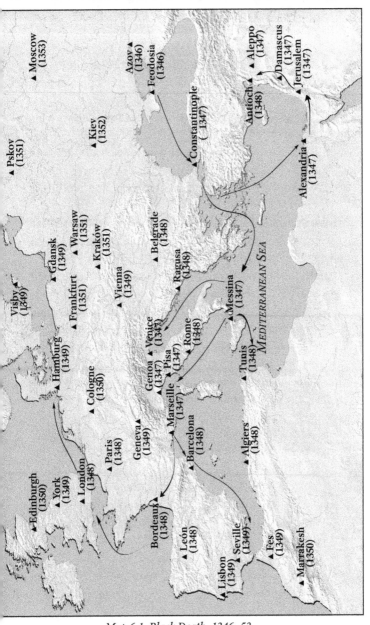

Map 6.1. Black Death, 1346–53.

respectively. Crusading within Latin Christendom also continued to be popular, whether against opponents of the papacy or against new "heresies."

The second part of the answer rests in the continuing appeal of the central ideological themes of crusading: the desire for spiritual benefits and salvation; the desire to expand Christendom and convert or eliminate perceived threats to it, both internal and external; and the desire to control lands deemed holy. Belief in the power and righteousness of sanctified violence undergirded these desires. Crusading also continued to draw strength from key cultural patterns: devotional practices, chivalry, family traditions. All these themes and patterns continued to prove adaptable and appealing to many different kinds of people. Crusading could be as useful to groups trying to enact social change from below as to powers trying to direct change from above or defend the status quo.

At the same time, crusading did not continue exactly as it had been. We can identify changes in both crusading ideas and practices in the late medieval and early modern period. First, crusading ideas were integrated with the ideals of late medieval humanism to produce what has been called "Renaissance crusading."[28] From this perspective, older themes like Christian unity and the defense and liberation of Christendom were joined by renewed calls for civic, educated, and rational action. Indeed, some of the key figures in the Renaissance—such as Petrarch—were crusade enthusiasts. For some, the

---

28 Norman Housley, *The Later Crusades, 1274–1580: From Lyons to Alcazar* (Oxford: Oxford University Press, 1992).

quest to reconnect with antiquity (and disconnect with the Middle Ages) was fueled by a desire to disavow any common intellectual heritage with the Islamicate world.

Second, people transferred crusading ideas more and more to national identities and conflicts. Of course, this was not an entirely new phenomenon. After all, Urban II had deliberately appealed to the Franks and their sense of Frankish identity when he preached in 1095; crusaders in 1188 wore different colored crosses to indicate English, Frankish, or Flemish identity; rulers had deliberately pursued crusading alongside territorial expansion and political aggrandizement in Iberia, northern Europe, and the eastern Mediterranean. But in the later Middle Ages, as European monarchs strengthened their positions and increasingly claimed to rule over distinct nations, the connection intensified. At the risk of oversimplifying a complicated relationship, whereas in the twelfth and early thirteenth centuries we might describe crusades as Latin Christian holy wars with national inflections, by the sixteenth century we might describe crusades as national holy wars rooted in a Latin Christian tradition.

Strengthened ideological connections between states, nationhood, and crusading could be seen in crusading practices, too. First, in this later period we see the emergence of order-states: political entities governed by military orders. These polities were Latin Christian theocracies in which a small elite, composed of fighting men from outside the region in question, governed a larger subject population. Second, we see the creation of crusade leagues: temporary alliances of nations committed to this or that crusading endeavor. No longer were crusades even nominally supranational; instead, they were an explicit expression of relations between nations.

***

In the early years of the fourteenth century, Latin Christians expressed dismay at the Mamluk conquest of Acre in 1291. Criticism centered on the multinational military orders. These orders were supposed to be dedicated to the maintenance, defense, and expansion of Christendom. They had become powerful and wealthy. Yet they seemed to have failed stupendously. As theoreticians tried to plan for a more successful crusading future, they envisioned uniting all military orders into one "super-order" led by a new warrior king of Jerusalem. While criticism of the pan-Mediterranean military orders was widespread, the Templars bore the brunt of it: the order was accused of heresy and ultimately suppressed, its assets dispersed.

The dissolution of the Templars in 1312 was not a sign of diminished crusading enthusiasm. On the contrary, the 1320s and early 1330s witnessed a strong revival of crusading enthusiasm across Europe. Philip IV of France was devoted to the legacy of crusading associated with his royal family, the Capetians, as well as with the family of his wife, Joan of Navarre, who was Philip's queen consort, the reigning queen of Navarre, and the reigning countess of Champagne. Philip made a sustained effort—using pomp, pageantry, propaganda, and thus significant funds—to rally both the French and the English for a crusade to the eastern Mediterranean. Yet he also brought charges against the Templars and successfully outfaced the papacy in the latest round of papal-regnal conflict in the early 1300s. The same monarch could pursue open conflict with the papacy and a major military order while simultaneously expressing substantial crusading fervor because both the conflict and the fervor could be, and were, represented as a concern for Christian piety. Thus it is perhaps not so surprising that other military orders, in particular the Hospitallers and Teutonic Knights, survived. They did so in part by establishing their usefulness, affirming their dual commitment to warfare and charitable works, and ensuring their political independence by establishing order-states.

The Teutonic Knights established semi-sovereign order-states in Prussia and Livonia and continued to successfully lead crusading in the Baltics. Recruitment of knights from elsewhere in Europe to fight on winter or summer campaigns was bolstered by the emergence of two new pagan enemies: the Mongols, and the Lithuanians, who had been unified by a confident and expansionist leader in the mid-thirteenth century. The chivalric accoutrements increasingly provided by the order also helped with recruitment. Participants in campaigns were honored in various ways. They could leave painted shields hanging in an order fortress, were ceremonially feasted, and on at least one occasion were presented with badges inscribed "honor conquers all."[29] Indeed, crusading in northern Europe only began petering out in the early

---

29 Riley-Smith, *Crusades*, 284.

fifteenth century, when it was undone by its own success in eliminating or converting its targets.

In the meantime, the Hospitallers had also established an order-state in the early 1300s, in their case on the island of Rhodes. They conquered Rhodes in 1309 and by the early 1320s their increased landholdings and possession of former Templar assets enabled them to maintain an active military role in the eastern Mediterranean. Rhodes itself—located on key maritime trade routes with a Greek-speaking populace—became a destination for a small number of European colonists. The Hospitallers fortified Rhodes extensively and by the early fifteenth century, the island was a vital entrepôt for both merchants and pilgrims in the Mediterranean. Meanwhile, its navy played a major role in Mediterranean crusading.

Eastern Mediterranean crusading in the fourteenth century pursued two related goals: defeating (or at least countering) the Mamluks and reestablishing a Latin Kingdom of Jerusalem. Leadership for these crusades was provided by a variety of lay powers, the Hospitallers, and the papacy. The monarchs of France and England and the Italian city-states and kingdoms were particularly enthusiastic in the promotion of crusading. So too was Peter I of Cyprus, who, as noted, reignited hopes for a major expedition to take Jerusalem in the very immediate aftermath of the Black Death. Various configurations of these leaders formed and reformed as crusade leagues, i.e., allied states devoted to a specific crusading endeavor.

Despite the time, energy, and resources thrown at eastern Mediterranean crusading in the fourteenth century, and despite temporary triumphs here and there, from a Latin Christian perspective it continued to be unsuccessful. As should sound familiar at this point, its failure can be traced to intra-Christian conflict and the military superiority of the Mamluks, as well as less predictable factors like a changing climate and plague. Furthermore, all parties in the eastern Mediterranean continued to be as frequently united as divided by economic interests. At times shared interests took prominence and calmed the waters for decades at a time, sometimes promoting Christian-Muslim alliances. For example, by 1490 the Kingdom of Cyprus had come to rest in the hands of the Venetians with the approval of the Mamluk sultan. He had recognized that his interests aligned with Venice much more closely than they did with the previous Frankish rulers of Cyprus, who had allowed their ports to become havens for pirates. As had always been the case, religious identity was only one factor among many.

Unsurprisingly, then, crusading by Latin Christians against Latin Christians also persisted in the fourteenth century. The papacy remained concerned about the conflict of interest between themselves and various rulers. Not even the fourteenth-century removal of the papacy and papal curia to Avignon in France—known as the Avignon Papacy—ended these crusades within western Europe. On the contrary, the perceived vulnerability of and threats to the papacy further motivated popes to use crusading against their adversaries. The same would prove true when the Latin Church was divided by the Great (Western) Schism from 1378–1417.

You might think that all this crusading would have used up even the most widespread enthusiasm, but crusading in Iberia continued to attract devotees in the fourteenth century. Not much headway was made by Latin Christian rulers in Iberia, though it appeared that might change in the middle of the century. In 1340 the Marinids began to actively move troops across from north Africa to assail Latin Christian targets. Alfonso XI of Castile, who was quite militarily adept, managed to counter the Marinids' moves, igniting support within Europe more broadly. But in the end, the Marinids were deprived of their adversary by the Black Death; Alfonso died of plague while besieging Granada in 1350. The Kingdom of Granada would remain firmly installed for another hundred years or so.

In the meantime, Latin Christian ambitions in Iberia turned, or rather returned, towards Africa. North Africa was both strategically and economically important, both in and of itself and as a route to the wealthy and globally interconnected societies of both west and east Africa. As a result, the region had long been coveted by European powers who had planned and at times executed various crusades against Islamicate powers in the region. With the stalemate over Granada, Peter I of Castile proposed to act on those intentions in 1354. Four decades later, in 1390, crusading in north Africa—in this case, against Mahdia in what is now Tunisia—would prove alluring enough to transcend the Great (Western) Schism and generate a multinational force.

In the early fifteenth century, two factors drove even greater crusade enthusiasm in Latin Christendom: the end of the Great (Western) Schism in 1417, which seemed

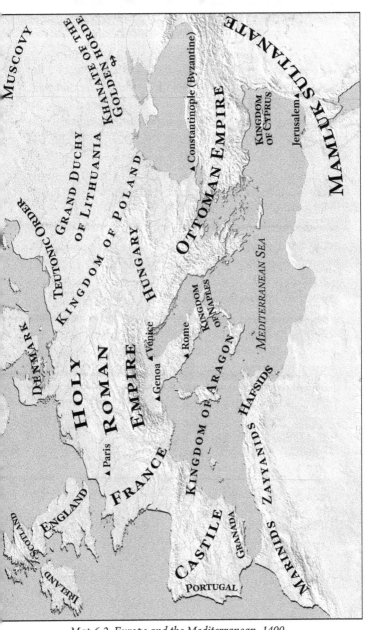

Map 6.2. Europe and the Mediterranean, 1400.

to signal the restoration of Latin Christian unity, and the increasingly undeniable strength of the Ottoman Turks. Yet this heightened enthusiasm was not at first directed towards the Ottomans. Instead, it was channeled into "the last great series of crusades against heretics,"[30] the five Hussite crusades in Bohemia (*ca.* 1419 to 1434). The very same ecclesiastical council resolved the Great (Western) Schism and condemned Jan Hus to be burned at the stake for heresy. But the Hussite "heresy" itself, which condemned church corruption and argued forcefully for church and social reform (as many purported heresies did), continued to thrive even after Hus's death. In particular, its continued dominance in the Kingdom of Bohemia was fueled by connections between the "heretics'" religious beliefs and Czech nationalist sentiments. In 1419, Holy Roman Emperor-elect Sigismund of Luxemburg, one of the individuals who had helped condemn Jan Hus, inherited the right to the throne of Bohemia. Much to his chagrin, he was not welcomed by those who viewed him as a traitor to both Hus and the Czech people. With the support of the papacy, Sigismund and his allies began "the most futile"[31] and ineffective Hussite crusades.

From a historian's perspective, the Hussite crusades echoed certain aspects of earlier crusades against heretics like the Albigensian Crusades. In particular, they recalled the way that royal and papal power had combined to combat unorthodox religious beliefs that threatened the religio-political status quo, and the way that local

---

30 Riley-Smith, *Crusades*, 306.

31 Riley-Smith, *Crusades*, 307.

communities could and did effectively fight back against encroachment that they perceived as territorial and opportunistic. In addition, though, the Hussite crusades point us forwards towards sixteenth-century crusading. As Christopher Tyerman has underscored, the Hussites' "mixture of political, social and religious rebellion forged a potent threat."[32] Crusading could be a way for the lowest social classes to rebel against the powerful and the status quo, as seen before with the Crusade of the Shepherds in France (1251) and later with the Pilgrimage of Grace in England (1536). Nonetheless, to many Latin Christians in the early fifteenth century, the Hussite crusades began to look like a dangerous diversion from a far bigger threat: the Ottomans.

If we remain at a historical distance, the story of the Ottomans resembles the story of the Saljuqs: a story of an originally mobile Turkic people, led by a series of charismatic and effective leaders, who thought and fought their way to territorially-bound imperial greatness in west Asia, one of the eastern hemisphere's key crossroads. Purportedly inspired by a divine vision, Osman and his successors first solidified their position in Anatolia in the early fourteenth century. Their neighbor, the resurgent Byzantine Empire, was troubled by persistent conflicts over the imperial throne, and Osman's heirs rightly sensed opportunity. They offered their support as reliable and effective mercenary troops to this or that Byzantine contender. At the time, there were also larger conflicts taking shape in the Mediterranean. Around the middle of

32 Tyerman, *God's War*, 902.

the fourteenth century—in the midst of the Black Death—
the Byzantines became embroiled in the Venetian-
Genoese War (1350–55). Here, too, the Ottomans played
a role; they allied with Genoa against Byzantium and
Venice. Thus through a combination of diplomacy and
military skill the Ottomans expanded their own holdings
in the northeastern Mediterranean, steadily moving the
boundary of their lands westward into the Balkans.

The Ottomans' westward moves were eventually
viewed with alarm by Latin Christians in the second half
of the fourteenth century. Opposition was led by the
self-proclaimed power in the Balkans, the Kingdom of
Hungary. Yet Ottoman expansion was, in fact, halted by
an ambitious Muslim leader: Timur (known in European
sources as Timur the Lame or Tamerlane). Timur's
outwardly spiraling series of conquests in central Asia
eventually led to assaults on both Ottoman and Mamluk
towns in the late fourteenth and early fifteenth centuries.
It would not be until the mid-fifteenth century that the
Ottomans again unified under one ruler (Murad II,
r. 1421–44 and 1446–51), consolidating their holdings in
Anatolia and hungering for further expansion.

Murad II, like so many other rulers we've looked at,
operated through a combination of diplomacy (including
marriage) and force. He also recognized that his human
obstacles were diverse: other Islamicate powers, such
as the Mamluks; the Byzantine Empire; and various
European powers, notably Hungary and Venice, who
were most active and ambitious in the northeastern
Mediterranean. Under Murad's rule, the Ottomans
successfully held off—arguably, defeated—the Hungarians

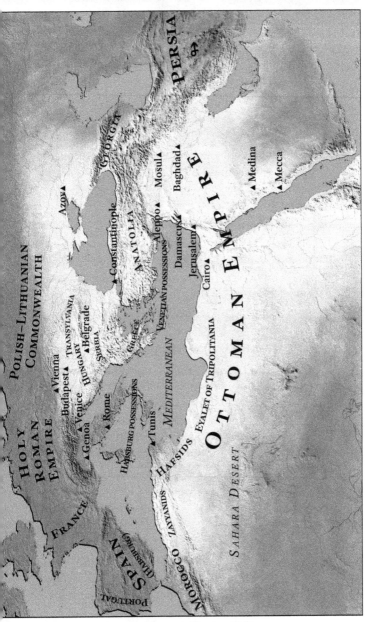

Map 6.3. Ottoman Empire, 1566.

and their allies, despite the crusading enthusiasm that swelled the Hungarians' ranks.

With Hungary and Venice firmly held at arms' length, Murad's heir, Mehmed II, turned to tackle the Byzantine Empire, conquering Constantinople in 1453 with a notable combination of military strategy and technology. Mehmed's great-grandson, Selim, would in turn mop up the Mamluks, taking Cairo in 1517. Hospitaller Rhodes fell to the Ottomans in 1522—and still, Ottoman expansion into eastern Europe, west Asia, and Africa continued. By 1566, the Ottoman Empire sprawled across three continents, blanketing the crucial trade routes connecting Europe, east Africa, and west Asia. The empire would only come to an end in the early 1920s.

Ottoman successes in the fifteenth century prompted waves of crusade enthusiasm in Latin Christendom, especially after the Ottoman conquest of Constantinople in 1453. Expeditions were planned and attracted not only the rich and powerful but also the poor. Few actually set out and virtually all faced the same old challenges: inadequate unification, underestimation and/or misunderstanding of the enemy's situation, and insufficient military strength. The lack of crusade success in the fifteenth century used to be read as a lack of interest in crusading, but in fact, crusading enthusiasm was being harnessed in European national interests like never before, and this, too, was part of the reason for crusading failure against the Ottomans.

The gold standard example of this was in the Iberian peninsula. After smoldering for nearly a century, crusading in Iberia flamed high when the kingdoms of Aragon and Castile were joined by the marriage of

Ferdinand II of Aragon and Isabella I of Castile in 1479. Led by the capable and ambitious Isabella, the now-united Spanish threw themselves (and all the help they could recruit from the rest of Latin Christendom) against the Kingdom of Granada. Undermined by its own internal disputes and overwhelmed by the Spanish onslaught, Granada surrendered in 1492.

As noted, crusading was driven by success as well as failure, and thus the successful conquest of Granada inspired an invasion of Africa starting in 1497. In this, the Spanish were not innovating, but rather following the example of Portugal, which had been crusading in north Africa since the early fifteenth century. The Spanish turned also to the lands that would become known to Europeans as the Americas. Isabella and Ferdinand sponsored Christopher Columbus, a crusade enthusiast who wrote that his "successes" in the western hemisphere were consolation for the "matter of the Holy Sepulchre."[33]

The efforts in Africa, in particular, were crusades, but they were national crusades—they were framed in terms of Spanish national identity, national sponsorship, national gain, national expansion, at the same time as they continued to refer to Christendom's gain and expansion. They were supported by national military orders, which were subject to national rather than papal authority. To be most accurate, we should say that this was Christian nationalism, informed by a crusading past and continuing to fuel territorial expansion in the early modern era.

33 Tyerman, *God's War*, 914.

It also fueled both local and national expulsions of Jews and Muslims throughout the Latin-ruled Mediterranean. The period from the twelfth century onwards had witnessed a crescendo of forcible expulsions and other forms of persecution, including, in 1516, the creation of the first Jewish ghetto in Venice. The same period saw the enslavement and expulsion of Muslim individuals and communities from Iberia and Italy. For those able to migrate, the Ottoman Empire became a refuge.

The other reason why crusading against the Ottomans was never successful is that the situation was always complex. As before, relationships in the Mediterranean could not be reductively characterized as "us vs. them." The Ottomans were Muslim, and they had conquered "Christian" lands, but they were also in control of key trade routes, which were used by European merchants (who contributed to the prosperity of their own locales). Furthermore, Ottoman rulers were intellectual, artistic, wealthy, interested in the transcultural exchange of ideas and goods, and relatively tolerant of their Jewish and Christian subjects. Not simply competitors or enemies, for many Latins engaged in the Mediterranean world, the Ottomans were resources, patrons, and allies. The precedent of military alliances between the Ottomans and Latin Christian powers had been set as early as the fourteenth century, as noted, and was cemented in place in the fifteenth century. Indeed, for some contemporary observers outside the Ottoman Empire (and certainly for many within its boundaries), the Ottomans had "inherited Roman universal sovereignty."[34]

In the early sixteenth century, outward-facing crusading continued in north Africa, on the frontiers of Hungary, and in the eastern Mediterranean. Crusading thus continued to be a multi-front phenomenon. On all three fronts, crusading enthusiasm fused with national interests to prompt wars driven by explicitly Christian national sentiment. Drawing on centuries of intra-Christian crusading, such crusades could be easily levied against other Christian-led nations. They could also be aimed at purported heresies—and the new "heresies" sweeping Europe starting in the sixteenth century alarmed many. From a historical perspective, of course, these "heresies" were the Protestant Reformations.

Crusades against Protestants were called for, and not only by the powerful or the popes; in the 1530s, rebels of many classes who opposed Henry VIII of England and his religious agenda wore crusading badges during the rebellion they called the "Pilgrimage of Grace." And although Protestants denied the papacy any right to wage war, many of them nonetheless embraced the idea of Christian holy war. Indeed, both Catholics and Protestants rhetorically linked war against each other with war against "the Turk." This usually meant that both one's Christian opponent and the Ottomans were perceived as enemies, but in a crisis, the Ottomans might even be considered the lesser of two evils; for example, Pope Paul IV allied with the Ottomans against his imperial adversaries,

---

34 Housley, *Later Crusades*, 97.

the Habsburgs.[35] Once again, we are reminded that the history of the crusades does not always conform to fault lines expected in the modern era.

Was crusading on its way out? This is a difficult question to answer. In the later Middle Ages and the beginning of the early modern period, crusading as a cultural phenomenon remained attractive to Latin Christians and was acted upon at different social levels, though admittedly the most effective enterprises were led by the powerful. Crusading in the eastern Mediterranean was as ineffective as ever, but crusading elsewhere was remarkably successful and helped ensure a strong link between crusading and national identities. One potential end date for crusading was 1572, when Pope Pius IV declared the last multinational crusade accompanied by a grant of remission of sins to participants. Thus perhaps we can say that after 1600, wars of Christian nationalism replaced crusading. However, in 1645 crusade indulgences were granted to those who defended Crete against the Ottomans. Pushing the timeline even farther is the fact that while the Hospitallers had been displaced from Rhodes by the Ottomans, they reestablished their order-state on Malta in 1530 and remained there, a theocracy under the rule of their grand-master and committed to their military role, until 1798. As the conclusion discusses, the question of when the history of the crusades ends and the memory of the crusades begins is complicated and contentious.

---

35 Riley-Smith, *Crusades*, 319.

Further Reading

Barber, Malcolm. *The Trial of the Templars*. 2nd ed. Cambridge: Cambridge University Press, 2012.

Campbell, Bruce M. *The Great Transition: Climate, Disease and Society in the Late-Medieval World*. Cambridge: Cambridge University Press, 2016.

Casale, Giancarlo. *The Ottoman Age of Exploration*. Oxford: Oxford University Press, 2011.

Einbinder, Susan L. *No Place of Rest: Jewish Literature, Expulsion, and the Memory of Medieval France*. Philadelphia: University of Pennsylvania Press, 2008.

Green, Monica H., ed. *Pandemic Disease in the Medieval World: Rethinking the Black Death*. Kalamazoo: ARC Medieval Press, 2015.

Grieve, Patricia E. *The Eve of Spain: Myths of Origins in the History of Christian, Muslim, and Jewish Conflict*. Baltimore: Johns Hopkins University Press, 2009.

Hashmi, Sohail M., ed. *Just Wars, Holy Wars, and Jihads: Christian, Jewish, and Muslim Encounters and Exchanges*. Oxford: Oxford University Press, 2012.

Housley, Norman. *The Later Crusades, 1274–1580: From Lyons to Alcazar*. Oxford: Oxford University Press, 1992.

Kafadar, Cemal. *Between Two Worlds: The Construction of the Ottoman State*. Berkeley and Los Angeles: University of California Press, 1995.

Ozment, Steven. *The Age of Reform, 1250–1550: An Intellectual and Religious History of Late Medieval and Reformation Europe.* New Haven, CT: Yale University Press, 1981.

Conclusion:
Have the Crusades
Ended?

"'Crusade' even in its most apparently benign usage
divides the world into black and white [...] it effaces
the nuance, the grey, in both our modern world and
the medieval one it purports to represent."[36]

CRUSADING INFLUENCED EUROPEAN NATIONAL
identities and European interactions with the rest of the
world in the early modern and modern eras. This lasting
impression is visible in not only the material cultures of
Europe and in a legacy of anti-Jewish and anti-Muslim
ideologies and actions, but in European philosophy
and history. In eighteenth-century Europe, historians
like David Hume and Edward Gibbon disparaged the

36 Matthew Gabriele, "Debating the 'Crusade' in Contemporary
America," *The Medieval Journal* 6: 1 (2016): 84.

crusades as the opposite of the rational "Enlightenment" they themselves hoped to promote. This disparagement created an image of the crusades that has persisted to the present, namely, that of barbaric wars fueled by greed and religious fanaticism. From this perspective, these unholy wars serve as the mascot for a murky Middle Ages, a veritable Dark Age. In creating this image of the crusades, eighteenth-century historians pulled on medieval sources selectively, making use of those that supported their perspective and ignoring—or unaware of—counterevidence.

In contrast, nineteenth-century romanticism and nationalism ushered in an era of increased positive attention to the crusades in Europe. Romantic writers like Sir Walter Scott and William Wordsworth simultaneously glorified both the crusades and Salah al-Din, whom they depicted as culturally and morally sophisticated. Historians like Joseph Michaud used the crusades to bolster contemporary national identity and kindle nationalistic fervor. The great edited compilations of crusading primary sources were constructed at the same time as the great edited compilations of "national" primary sources from the Middle Ages, and some imperialists explicitly linked their enterprises to earlier centuries of crusading. For example, L'Institut Religieux et Militaire des Frères Armés du Sahara, a new military order, was briefly created to promote Franco-Catholic interests in Africa, while in England, Sir William Hillary called for a new crusade to seize Acre from the Ottomans and establish a new order-state centered on Jerusalem.

Unsurprisingly, then, in the nineteenth-century the English word "crusade" acquired the broader, romanticized meaning of a righteous pursuit of justice. The romantic nationalists had generated a second image of the crusades that has also persisted to the present. Thus, in European history and memory, the eighteenth-century image of unholy holy wars rubbed shoulders with the nineteenth-century image of honorable, glorious, and self-sacrificing quests to build a better world by using force to smite the evildoer, defend the good, and liberate the oppressed. In creating this nineteenth-century image of the crusades, European historians, like their eighteenth-century predecessors, used medieval sources selectively.

The crusades continued to be invoked as an historical example for imperialist and other national or "Western" military endeavors in the twentieth century. Jonathan Riley-Smith has asserted that it was in the aftermath of World War I that European nations and the United States of America drew back from explicit comparison between modern warfare and the crusades.[37] However, such comparisons actually carried on later into the twentieth century; examples are as readily available as President Dwight D. Eisenhower's 1948 memoir of World War II, titled *Crusade in Europe*.[38] Indeed, in the early twenty-first century American politicians on both right and left have continued to discuss "crusading" either to support

37 Riley-Smith, *Crusades*, 344.
38 See also, particularly, Rick Atkinson, *Crusade: The Untold Story of the Persian Gulf War* (New York: Houghton Mifflin, 1993).

or criticize American aggression.[39] Meanwhile, as Andrew Elliott has demonstrated, the crusades are heavily invoked and reimagined by white nationalists across mass media platforms.[40]

In Islamicate spheres, the crusades have also been remembered in different ways and used to support different contemporary agendas. Memories of the crusades and of Salah al-Din in particular, as well as "fears of renewed attack," remained present in Islamic popular and historical literature.[41] These memories were influenced—though not caused—by European cultural trends in the nineteenth century; the romanticized vision of bold yet culturally unsophisticated crusaders encountering a superior and chivalric Salah al-Din was particularly in line with existing trends in Islamic historiography.

The fall of the Ottoman Empire after World War I gave rise to both Arab Nationalism and Pan-Islamism, which each remembered and reimagined the crusades. Both

---

39 Gabriele, "Debating the 'Crusade'."

40 Andrew B. R. Elliott, *Medievalism, Politics and Mass Media. Appropriating the Middle Ages in the Twenty-First Century* (Woodbridge: D. S. Brewer, 2017). See especially Chapters 4, 6, and 7.

41 Diana Abouali, "Saladin's Legacy in the Middle East," *Crusades* 10 (2011): 175–85, at 180. See also Konrad Hirschler, "The Jerusalem Conquest of 492/1099 in the Medieval Arabic Historiography of the Crusades: From Regional Plurality to Islamic Narrative," *Crusades* 13 (2014), 37–76.

Arab Nationalists and Pan-Islamists oppose American and European imperialism in its political and cultural dimensions and both movements seek to build a unified state in west Asia. Both also believe that such a state would reflect the history of the region accurately. In other words, from their perspective, such a state would constitute a return to a better model rather than an entirely unprecedented challenge to the imperialist status quo. However, at the risk of overgeneralizing, while Arab Nationalists seek to build a unified Arab nation, Pan-Islamists seek to build a unified Islamic nation, i.e., a theocracy. In the later twentieth century, speaking again in broad terms, Arab Nationalism lost ground to Pan-Islamism.

Both Arab Nationalists and Pan-Islamists have constructed and made use of their own images of the crusades. For mid-twentieth-century thinkers like Sayyid Qutb, the crusades were an ominous history, the victories of Salah al-Din notwithstanding. Western imperialism/intervention in majority Muslim regions—including, after World War II, the existence of the state of Israel—appeared as the latest manifestation of "Crusading Spirit."[42] Thus the crusades became both an inspirational example from the past and an ongoing and oppressive reality to fight in the present. Political leaders, perhaps most notably Gamal 'Abd al-Nasir, President of Egypt (1956–70), and Saddam Hussein, President of Iraq (1979–2003), used words, art, and in the case of al-Nasir, film to depict themselves as modern Salah al-Dins. While twenty-first-century

42 Qutb, *Social Justice in Islam*, 269.

militant groups like al Qaeda and IS do not share all the same goals and ideals, they do share anti-crusading rhetoric and imagery. Furthermore, they have effectively used references to crusading in American and European political discourse to bolster their claim that the crusades are indeed ongoing and require armed resistance.[43]

In summary, then, there are a number of modern actors worldwide who maintain that the crusades are ongoing today, even if they disagree on whether that is a reason to rejoice or an injustice to protest. Whether rejoicing or protesting, these modern actors often see the continuation of crusading as a reason to take up arms and commit violence. And strictly speaking, these actors are not completely fabricating the history of the crusades, but rather—not unlike European historians in the eighteenth and nineteenth centuries—they are seizing upon the evidence they want to see and disregarding the rest.

One might hope that a historian's perspective would be clearer, but even as a historian, it is difficult to establish a precise date at which the crusades can indeed be said to have ended. If we apply pluralist criteria, it appears that crusading ended in 1645. But the persistence of Hospitaller Malta into the eighteenth century and the nineteenth-century example of L'Institut Religieux et Militaire des Frères Armés du Sahara make it difficult to fix a concrete end date. Faced with this problem, Jonathan Riley-Smith suggested two analytical categories for modern phenomena: "para-crusading" (containing

---

43 Elliott, *Medievalism, Politics and Mass Media*, especially Chapters 5 and 8.

some "authentic elements") and "pseudo-crusading" (containing no "authentic elements," just borrowed rhetoric and imagery).[44] According to these categories, L'Institut Religieux et Militaire des Frères Armés du Sahara was paracrusading, while Eisenhower's choice of book title was pseudocrusading.

This analytical model is quite unwieldy but that very unwieldiness is illuminating. Clearly, even if we conclude that the crusades ended in the mid-seventeenth century, the legacy of crusading continues to unfold. As a result, crusading cannot be decisively locked into the box of the Middle Ages and the key thrown away; neither can modern violence, rhetorical or physical, be neatly detached from the premodern past. We are unavoidably challenged to contend with complex and contested ideas about the past alongside ongoing and horribly real violence in the present.

I hope to have shown in this book that the complicated nature of the crusades—the extreme multivalence of crusading—long predates the modern era's use of the term and the history. Crusading emerged from a long tradition of Christian violence and warfare, as well as within a dynamic Mediterranean world. Crusading was always viewed differently by different observers and participants, and even in the Middle Ages, its history was often linked to one political agenda or another. Those Latin Christians who supported crusading utilized a wide and variable set of ideas and cultural practices to do so. Those outside the cultural boundaries of Latin

44 Riley-Smith, *Crusades*, 333–36.

Christendom not only viewed the crusades in different ways, but viewed them in ways that shifted over time, as they variously found themselves allies or enemies of crusaders. On all sides, some deliberately presented and may well have fully believed in the crusading enterprise as a categorical civilizational conflict. Yet given the ways in which Latin Christians used crusading to further their own political, economic, and social causes, including against each other, and given the wide range of people who participated in crusading, it is impossible to claim that the crusades actually *were* categorical civilizational conflicts, or even that all of those involved believed them to be so. It is also impossible to claim that all the targets of crusading violence necessarily interpreted every assault they suffered as religious or cultural violence, as opposed to violence motivated by political or economic concerns. To emphatically quote historian Brian Catlos, "we should not expect the people of the past to be any more coherent, consistent, or comprehensible than those of today."[45]

When today the crusades are invoked in twenty-first-century geopolitics, they are usually invoked, in the words of Umej Bhatia, as a "poster-child of civilizational conflict." To depict crusading in this way does draw upon some historical evidence—namely, the evidence that presents the crusades in that way—but simultaneously ignores the evidence for a much more complex and interconnected past. These depictions also draw upon

45 Brian A. Catlos, *Muslims of Medieval Latin Christendom, c. 1050–1614* (Cambridge: Cambridge University Press, 2014), 520.

all the images of crusading generated in the eighteenth, nineteenth, and twentieth centuries. In other words, when we look at how the crusades are used in contemporary geopolitics, we see both the influence of an incomplete interpretation of the medieval past *and* the influence of modern histories, ideologies, priorities, and practices. Historians can counter the selective interpretation of the past by providing a broader perspective, as this book has sought to do, but that broader perspective will remain full of complexity and ambiguity.

While recognizing that complexity and ambiguity can be frustrating, these characteristics of the history of the crusades may be uniquely valuable. Given the effectiveness of 'us vs. them' rhetorics of religious violence in the past and in the present, complexity and ambiguity seem particularly constructive. They encourage us to continue to ask questions, consider alternatives, rethink conclusions, and acknowledge complications. The very desire many clearly feel for crystalline clarity on the question of "the crusades"—at its most extreme, a desire for an 'us vs. them' past to support an 'us vs. them' present—should urge us to recognize the variety of ways in which history has been and still is mobilized for polemical purposes and to incite violence. I hope that this book leads you, the reader, to do all of these things as you continue to explore the history of crusading for yourself.

Further Reading

Bhatia, Umej. *Forgetting Osama bin Munqidh, Remembering Osama bin Laden: The Crusades in Modern Muslim Memory*. Singapore: S. Rajaratnam School of International Studies, 2008.

Elliott, Andrew B.R. *Medievalism, Politics and Mass Media. Appropriating the Middle Ages in the Twenty-First Century*. Woodbridge: D. S. Brewer, 2017.

Horswell, Mike, and Jonathan Phillips, eds. *Perceptions of the Crusades from the Nineteenth to the Twenty-First Century*. Oxon: Routledge, 2018.

Kayalı, Hasan. *Arabs and Young Turks: Ottomanism, Arabism and Islamism in the Ottoman Empire, 1908–1918*. Berkeley: University of California Press, 1997.

Wien, Peter. *Arab Nationalism. The Politics of History and Culture in the Modern Middle East*. London: Routledge, 2017.

Index

Credits

wiki/File:Al-idrisi_world_map.jpg>. The whole work can be viewed online on the Bibliothèque nationale de France's website: <https://gallica.bnf.fr/ark:/12148/btv1b6000547t.r=.langEN>; 3) a diagram of the four seasons and four cardinal directions, from a copy of Isidore's *De natura rerum*: London, British Library, Harley MS 3099, fol. 156ʳ: see <https://blogs.bl.uk/digitisedmanuscripts/2017/03/female-scribes-in-early-manuscripts-.html> and the whole manuscript on the British Library's website: <https://www.bl.uk/manuscripts/FullDisplay.aspx?ref=Harley_MS_3099>; 4) A world map from Leinhart Holle's 1482 edition of Ptolemy's *Geography*: Holle's entire *Cosmographia* may be viewed online at the Internet Archive: <https://archive.org/details/cosmographia00ptol>; the map can be found at <https://commons.wikimedia.org/wiki/File:Claudius_Ptolemy-_The_World.jpg>. The map goes back to Ptolemy (100–*ca*.170) via the Byzantine translator Maximus Planudes (*ca*.1260–*ca*.1305), the Italian humanist Jacobus Angelus/Jacopo d'Angelo (1360–1411), and German cartographer Nicolaus Germanus (*ca*.1420–*ca*.1490). Original images in the public domain, edited by Kısmet Press, and republished under the same license.

Maps are by Kısmet Press, based on those created by Koba-chan from the public domain DEMIS Mapserver. The full set may be found online here: <https://commons.wikimedia.org/wiki/Atlas_of_the_World/Physical_and_topographical>. These maps were released by Koba-chan under the CC BY-SA 3.0 license and the maps in this book are therefore released under the same license.

This sweeping yet succinct new survey introduces readers to the history of the crusades from the eleventh to the twenty-first century. By synthesizing a variety of historical perspectives, the book deliberately locates crusading in the broader history of the Mediterranean, moving away from approaches focused primarily on narrating the deeds of a small section of the Latin Christian elite to explore the rich and contested complexity of crusade history.

Susanna A. Throop is Associate Professor and Department Chair of History at Ursinus College. She is the author of *Crusading as an Act of Vengeance, 1095–1216*, and co-editor of *Vengeance in the Middle Ages: Emotion, Religion and Feud* and *The Crusades and Visual Culture*.

Kismet Press is a not-for-profit partnership committed to publishing high-quality, peer-reviewed works in the arts and humanities, and making them as accessible as possible, both in print and open access online.

kısmet·press

Libera Scientia | Free Knowledge

CPSIA information can be obtained
at www.ICGtesting.com
Printed in the USA
LVHW082238240820
664077LV00037B/3264